"At the frothy interface where high-tech radical concepts meet the deepest insights of religious tradition, Diana Pasulka raises the fundamental questions implicit in the new phenomena of space and nonhuman intelligence. Her message is plausible and urgent."

—Jacques Vallée, author of *Trinity: The Best-Kept Secret*

"This is a full-tilt roller coaster ride of an intellectual journey, as fascinating as it is frightening: a fast-paced plunge into the meta-media frenzy that has rewired the modern mind."

—Alan Steinfeld, author of *Making Contact*

"This is it. This is what I have been trying to say . . . In Pasulka's eloquent voice, religious studies becomes ufology, and ufology becomes religious studies. And both become more—way, way more."

—Jeffrey J. Kripal, author of *How to Think Impossibly*

"A clarion call for our technological age . . . Pasulka's prescience is combined with a master storytelling ability that is on full display here."

—Brett Robinson, PhD, associate director, McGrath Institute for Church Life, University of Notre Dame

"Pasulka is writing prophetically at the cutting edge of our accelerating culture. What she grapples with today, everyone else will be tomorrow. *The Others* is her most important book yet."

—Rod Dreher, author of *Living in Wonder* and *Live Not by Lies*

"An unsettling yet luminous meditation on technology, transcendence, and the sacred . . . This is not merely a book about the future, but a reckoning with unseen forces already reshaping our imagination and redefining what it truly means to be human." —Ryan Sprague, author and podcast host of *Somewhere in the Skies*

"A must-read for anyone interested in the rapid revolution occurring in our understanding of reality."
—The Honorable Tim Gallaudet, PhD

"Fascinating, erudite, and compulsively readable, this work offers clarity amid confusion and a sense of wisdom, meaning, hope, and humanity in a rapidly changing world."
—Joanna Ebenstein, founder and creative director of Morbid Anatomy

"At a time when AI is reshaping our world, and UAPs are dominating congressional hearings, Pasulka provides the intellectual framework we desperately need. *The Others* is the Rosetta stone for the strange new world we already inhabit." —Michael Shellenberger, bestselling author of *Apocalypse Never* and *San Fransicko*

"*The Others* is one of those rare books that doesn't try to shock you or force you into a conclusion. Instead, it feels like sitting down with someone thoughtful who's honestly trying to make sense of a very strange moment in history."
—Chad Hayes and Carey W. Hayes, writers, producers, and creators of the Conjuring franchise

THE OTHERS

ALSO BY D. W. PASULKA

Encounters: Experiences with Nonhuman Intelligences

American Cosmic: UFOs, Religion, Technology

Heaven Can Wait: Purgatory in Catholic Devotional and Popular Culture

THE OTHERS

UFOs, AI, and the Secret Forces Guiding Human Destiny

D. W. Pasulka

ST. MARTIN'S
ESSENTIALS
NEW YORK

First published in the United States by St. Martin's Essentials,
an imprint of St. Martin's Publishing Group

EU Representative: Macmillan Publishers Ireland Ltd, 1st Floor,
The Liffey Trust Centre, 117–126 Sheriff Street Upper, Dublin 1, D01 YC43

www.stmartins.com

Designed by Steven Seighman

The Library of Congress Cataloging-in-Publication Data
is available upon request.

ISBN 978-1-250-39486-6 (hardcover)
ISBN 978-1-250-39487-3 (ebook)

First Edition: 2026

10 9 8 7 6 5 4 3 2

To friend and colleague Jeffrey J. Kripal

CONTENTS

THE OTHERS

INTRODUCTION

DISRUPTIVE TRUTH

I teach my students about the biblical prophet Jonah. They know the basics of the story: He is the man who is swallowed by a big fish, spends three days in its belly, and gets spit out so he can tell the people of the town of Nineveh to change their ways. What my students don't know is that Jonah was a reluctant, angry prophet.

When God calls Jonah for help, Jonah immediately schemes a way to avoid the task and he runs away. God is inescapable, though, and Jonah soon realizes, while he is in the belly of the fish, that the only way out is to perform God's task. Begrudgingly, he goes to Nineveh where he explains to the people that unless they change their ways, God will annihilate them. Jonah is surprised when the king, upon hearing the news, immediately repents and issues a decree for the whole village that even extends to its cows:

> By the decree of the king and his nobles: No man or beast, herd or flock, is to taste anything; they are not to eat or drink. But let man and beast be covered with sackcloth. Let everyone call urgently on God. Let them give up their evil ways and their violence.[1]

Jonah was successful in his task and that should have made him happy. Instead, he is furious that God had mercy on the people in the kingdom. Exasperated, he leaves the village and goes to the desert and stews in his anger. God then causes a tree to grow and shade Jonah, and this gives him some respite. Then, God allows a worm to destroy the tree, and Jonah is exposed to the full force of the sun. He becomes angry again, and he even wishes he was dead.

"You are concerned about this plant," God says, "though you did not tend it or make it grow. . . . Should I not be concerned about Nineveh, that great city, in which there are more than 120,000 persons who do not know their right hand from their left—and also many animals?"[2]

The abrupt, odd end to the book inspired a long tradition of Christian and Jewish interpretations and questions. Why was Jonah reluctant to carry out God's task for him? Why was he upset when God proved to be merciful? Many recognized a cosmic message about God and his mercy. The people of Nineveh are described as wicked, but their wickedness stems from ignorance, not malice. Jonah would prefer to see them punished, not saved. God's saving mercy even extends to the nonhuman world.

The book emphasizes the prophet's reluctance and his pettiness when his mission succeeds. It also reveals that

God's mercy extends even to those whose wickedness arises from ignorance rather than intent. Finally, it affirms that the ways of God surpass human understanding, and embrace not only people, but all of creation.

And so it goes with prophets. They mostly carry the burden of their obligation with reluctance. In mythic terms, Jonah's story is not just about obedience to God but about the inescapable demand of revelation and truth itself. The visionary resists, and yet is chosen; he flees, and yet is found. From ancient prophets to modern witnesses of the extraordinary, the pattern repeats: Disruptive truth pursues those who would rather refuse it.

The Book of Jonah is not only about a prophet and a city. It dramatizes a theme: The most disruptive truths often arrive through flawed, reluctant messengers. Jonah flees, sulks, and even resents his own success, yet his words change the course of a civilization. God's mercy extends to those Jonah least wants to include—wicked people, enemies, even animals—and Jonah is left upset and confused that reality has outstripped his own categories of justice.

This pattern repeats across history. Visionaries and prophets are rarely the people we would choose as reliable guides. They are eccentric, marginalized, and ridiculed. Yet, like Jonah, they carry messages that change history. Debates around unidentified aerial phenomena (UAP), or UFOs, and artificial intelligence (AI) bear this stamp. The figures who raise uncomfortable questions, like the scientists at the margins, experiencers, abductees, and visionaries, are dismissed by mainstream science and culture. Like Jonah, they are often reluctant messengers. And like the king of Nineveh, powerful institutions now take notice of them.

The lesson of Jonah is that disruptive truth does not arrive on our terms. It arrives through strange, unwilling prophets and unsettles our categories of what counts as credible. It forces us to ask whether, like Jonah, we would rather cling to our skepticism than confront truths that exceed our understanding.

CATHOLIC VISIONARIES AND SCIENCE FICTION

We are living through a moment that earlier generations could only imagine. Artificial intelligence is reshaping how we live, and reports of nonhuman intelligence are regularly debated in US congressional hearings. This book focuses on a group of visionaries from the first half of the twentieth century who anticipated this moment: Pierre Teilhard de Chardin, René Girard, Marshall McLuhan, and Mark Stahlman—the only living member of the group. Formed within a Catholic intellectual tradition, these thinkers produced insights that now appear unmistakably prophetic. Each foresaw transformations in human culture, technology, and spirituality that have become fully legible only in the contemporary age of AI and UFOs. They described what is now visibly unfolding. Alongside them stands Arthur C. Clarke, who was not conventionally religious, but whose science fiction novel *Childhood's End* offers a popular culture rendering of the same future these visionaries anticipated.

Together, these figures described the emergence of a new human being, one inseparable from technology. Marshall McLuhan was a scholar of media technology, and he described this as a *supraterrestrial* order. Pierre Teilhard de Chardin, a Catholic priest and paleontologist, described the new human as the *Ultra-human* who would be connected to the *noosphere*: a planetary layer of cognition overlaying the biosphere, energized by technology, new economic forms, and shared thought. McLuhan argued that technological environments shape human consciousness, making his supraterrestrial a close echo of Chardin's noosphere. Clarke's *Childhood's End* is the fictional version of these predictions, as it depicts children absorbed into an alien hive mind—a transformation that tragically severs them from their parents and inaugurates a new form of human being.

Each of these thinkers, in different ways, reveals an era that inaugurates a new evolutionary step for humanity—one that brings the current form of the human to an end. Although Clarke's vision is fictional, both Chardin and McLuhan believed they were witnessing the dawn of a new kind of human being.

What these visionaries described finds a parallel in the testimonies surrounding UFOs. Such encounters gesture toward forms of intelligence irreducible to human categories. To some they appear technological; to others, manifestations of a nonhuman or more-than-human agency. What is most striking, however, is that UFOs are more complicated than what is shown in popular media. They may appear as discs moving at impossible speeds, turning at sharp angles, or defying the known laws of physics. Yet they also shape-shift:

They appear as glowing lights to one observer and as immense structured craft to another. Communication often occurs not through language but through mental impressions, visions, or sudden floods of information.

Many years ago, I met Dr. Jacques Vallée. Known both as a computer scientist and a ufologist, Vallée worked in the 1970s on the Advanced Research Projects Agency Network (ARPANET), the proto-internet that laid the foundation for today's digital networks. At the same time, he pursued research on UFOs, compiling cases that challenged the conventional "nuts-and-bolts spacecraft" narrative. When I met Jacques, I sensed that these two domains, computer networking and the study of anomalous phenomena, were not coincidental in his life, though I did not fully grasp their connection.

Over time, the picture clarified. Both ARPANET and the UFO phenomena point to distributed intelligence. The internet functions as a graph, each node (computer) capable of transmitting and transforming information without a central point of control. Vallée suggested that UFOs behave in a strikingly similar fashion: not as singular craft from a distant planet, but as an information system, a network of signs and encounters that adapt to and change the cultural expectations of those who witness it.

UFOS AND TECHNOLOGY

Vallée's vision, and that of other ufologists like John Keel, resonates with McLuhan's theories and Chardin's noosphere.

All point to a time in which intelligence transcends the human, structures reality in ways that we dimly perceive, and suggests a form of propaganda or control. Both Clarke and McLuhan reveal that media technologies are control mechanisms. The control mechanism hypothesis is not new. Approximately twenty-four hundred years ago, the philosopher Plato described the details of social control in his book *The Republic*. What is new is that today these mechanisms are inseparable from technological systems, and that the architecture of media itself can be coded for control and persuasion—for ends that could be good or bad.

The visionaries ascribed different names to a similar idea—a new form of human being created through a technologically saturated environment. They also predicted a similar time frame, the early twenty-first century. This is the time when artificial intelligence has been introduced as a disruptive and life-changing advancement. At the same time, after *The New York Times*'s 2017 article "Glowing Auras and 'Black Money': The Pentagon's Mysterious U.F.O. Program," UFOs make weekly headline news around the world. We are now confronted with realities that once were the stuff of science fiction: technological enhancement of the human being, artificial intelligence that appears humanlike, the extension of the human lifespan, and a potential interface with nonhuman intelligence.

AI creators and commentators, from Ethan Mollick to Yuval Noah Harari, insist that artificial intelligence is no longer just a tool but a new order of intelligence. Harari even recasts the acronym itself, calling AI "alien intelligence." Mollick underscores the same point: "We have created something that has convinced many smart people that it is, in some way, the spark of a new form of intelligence. An AI that has blown through . . . the Turing Test . . . an AI that aces our hardest exams." Harari adds: "It thinks, makes decisions and processes information in a fundamentally different way than humans."[3]

Unlike past technologies, AI develops on an exponential curve rather than a linear one, which means it will exceed our capacity to understand it far sooner than we expect. As one AI tech explained, "Human beings cannot comprehend exponential growth."

In the early twenty-first century, this is no longer speculation. AI has emerged as a disruptive, potentially world-altering form of intelligence, while UFOs have moved from the cultural fringe into mainstream headlines. And strikingly, the testimonies of experiencers of UFO events often echo the visionaries' narratives: encounters with intelligences that challenge the boundaries of the human.

If AI represents intelligence emerging from within our own tools, UFOs represent intelligence erupting from beyond. Both challenge assumptions that humanity is the sole measure of mind, and together they demand new categories of discernment.

This is where it is instructive to return to the visionaries, and Jonah. They share a focus on a spiritual sense—an interface with the sacred that in Jonah's case is represented as God speaking directly to him. The philosopher Aristotle (384–322 BCE) addresses a sense of "soul" (*psyche*), which the medieval scholastic Thomas Aquinas (1225–1274) later elaborates and reframes as a set of spiritual faculties that allow human beings to perceive spiritual realities. For Aquinas, the spiritual senses are as real as sight or touch and act as access points for sacred knowledge. The knowledge of and practices associated with training the spiritual senses have generally been passed down through traditional religions, but this has disappeared from common knowledge and even in most of these traditions. Mark Stahlman, whose mission, in part, is to revive knowledge about this tradition, argues that AI will force human beings to recognize that the capacity to connect to the sacred is what will ultimately differentiate AI from the human being. As Mark says, "The human being is oriented toward the transcendent. That is what makes them human."

With regard to UFOs, Jonah's story is also instructive. The scientists, experiencers, and scholars who have worked to study them since the 1950s and '60s have carried their task under a cloud of stigma. They operate in a strange twilight: entrusted with the highest levels of security clearances and asked to direct classified research programs, yet ridiculed or dismissed whenever their work becomes known outside those circles. For years I was among those who scoffed, and I don't blame others who still scoff. Yet, even the most cursory look into the topic uncovers a parallel tradition of inquiry—hidden from public view, supported by governments, and consistently met with derision when disclosed. The discomfort for these researchers is profound: to be indispensable on the inside and discredited on the outside. And the obvious question arises: If they are truly misguided, why would the US government invest in them, fund them, and place them in charge of classified programs?

A ROAD MAP TO THE BOOK

The book begins with the work of René Girard, a French academic who, through the course of his research into the classics of the Western tradition, converted to Catholicism. Girard is not the most dramatic of the visionaries, but his contribution is the most crucial. He holds a mirror to the past and present and reveals the patterns of violence and desire that govern much of human interaction. In doing so, he warns us of what lies ahead. His theory may lack the allure of Chardin and McLuhan, but it remains the most indispensable to understand.

A cherished goal of civil society has been the creation of an empathy-based culture where social relations are governed by the Golden Rule. Yet empathy does not arise automatically; many religious traditions hold that it is cultivated through a spiritual faculty which involves the capacity to perceive and respond to the dignity of others. If the architecture of AI is left to corporate interests, that faculty will atrophy, and with it the very basis of civil society. Norbert Wiener, the founder of cybernetics, which is the science of feedback theory and signal processing, warned, "If we use, to achieve our purposes, a mechanical agency with whose operation we cannot efficiently interfere . . . we had better be quite sure that the purpose put into the machine is the purpose which we really desire."[4] Without discernment, machines will scale our worst impulses into systems of violence.

Wiener's own experience illustrates the peril. A techno-optimist radicalized by his wartime work for the US military in the 1940s, he became increasingly alarmed as he realized that the systems he designed could—and would—escape human control. Today we might call him a doomer. His vacillation between enthusiasm and dread mirrors the ambivalence of the Catholic visionaries in this book: hopeful about technological possibility, horrified by its destructive capacity. Only Clarke maintained unshaken optimism. Girard, Chardin, McLuhan, and even Wiener, in different registers, all recognized that humanity approaches an apocalyptic horizon in which technological power will confront us with the necessity of what some have called a sanctifying grace. Wiener's last books were about religion and morality. Girard's insistence on personal sanctity and Wiener's sober warning about machines without moral oversight converge: They imply that only a society whose members have developed a spiritual sense can guide us through what lies ahead.

The book also features the experiences of people who have had anomalous encounters that they associate with UFOs. The "Starseed" transmissions that circulated in the 1970s have a second life among modern Cosmists, who speak of being drafted by cosmic intelligences to push human longevity and to train for life beyond Earth.

The spiritual sense achieves the status of a character in the book as the religious visionaries as well as the people featured attest to its action in their lives. While every culture has built tools that shape how it encounters the sacred, like icons, cathedrals, radio, movies, etc., the inner ability to perceive the sacred has remained the same. Injury, drugs, and trauma could distort this sense in individuals; thus most religious traditions advocate for a care of the body as a means to protect this sense or faculty. For the first time in human history, technology will potentially reshape this faculty across entire populations.

With the exception of Mark Stahlman, the visionaries in these pages have been revered and reviled—celebrated as holy, condemned as heretical, accused of racism or sexism. I will not defend them; rather, I regard their visions of the future as forms of perception that anticipated modern developments. Jonah was an imperfect human being, yet he warned the people of Nineveh that they were in danger of annihilation, and for that, they were grateful.

1

THE ANTICHRIST ALGORITHM

THE BALL

Flying through clear blue skies, I arrived in Miami for Hereticon—an exclusive, invitation-only gathering of so-called heretics. Named in honor of history's game-changers, the conference celebrated outlier thinkers whose ground-breaking ideas had reshaped cultures, often at great personal cost. In earlier eras, such innovators were often burned, murdered, or, at best, shunned and ignored. Hereticon set out to reverse that fate, creating a space to honor today's iconoclasts rather than banish them.

When I arrived, I was immediately impressed with the surreal blend of avant-garde spectacle with cutting-edge presentations. The event was sponsored by Peter Thiel's Founders Fund, and the theme for the year was "Apocalypse," a topic that was very much on my mind. This was not an academic conference, nor was it just a conference for people interested in extending their business networks. One of the featured attractions was a black-tie ball. The invitation instructed attendees to wear clothes befitting the apocalypse. I attended the first night's dinner with my friend, a mild-mannered scientist. As we walked to the dining room, we passed beautiful, barely clothed people posing as Aztec gods and goddesses. Live boa constrictors draped around their necks and bodies, and they posed with attendees for viral-worthy social media photos.

The event was a feast not just for the eyes, but also for the mind. Another friend and colleague, a high-ranking military official, was there at my request. We were there to present about the topic of UFOs. As he took in the scenery, he turned to me and said, "I've never been to a conference like this. On the plus side, every person I've spoken with has been smart." I nodded in agreement.

Months prior to the event, I had begun to feel like the frog in a slowly heating pot—too acclimated, too anesthetized, to notice the rising temperature until it was too late. The frog tale serves as a silent warning: The most dangerous changes unfold so gradually that their red flags go unnoticed. By October 2024, apocalyptic themes had woven themselves into every conversation. Even my atheist friends spoke of the upcoming US presidential election in terms of the end times. In its first-century Greek usage, *apocalypse*, or *apokálypsis*, meant an "unveiling" or "disclosure," a pulling back of the veil to reveal what was hidden. Set against the backdrop of the Aztec deities, I waited for Thiel's keynote, ominously titled "Antichrist," with the sense that this gathering was not heralding a single moment of cataclysm, but rather something more insidious: a relentless, almost imperceptible shift in our collective reality.

In this charged atmosphere where myth and modernity collided, my scientist friend was flashed by a beautiful stranger. I had made note of the stranger when I saw her out of the corner of my eye as we first arrived for dinner. I felt that she seemed too interested in us as we explored the ornate, Masonic-themed halls of the hotel. When I saw her again, I turned my head and looked away. My friend was not so lucky, or, depending on how one thought about these things, he was lucky. In any case, the brief moment shocked him but also prepared him for the unexpected. I had spent the weeks preceding the conference convincing him to attend, and although I felt a tinge of guilt that by being at the conference he would travel outside his comfort zone, I knew that the trip would be worthwhile. Neither of us had expected this type of revealing, however.

The next day, we all gathered in a sumptuous theater where Thiel was scheduled to speak. Anticipating a full house, we arrived early, but even then, we barely found seats near the periphery of the stage. The event began with a stylized, burlesque film that was an homage to Thiel's life and work, tongue-in-cheek in tone but precise in detail. It chronicled his role in launching the foundational digital platforms of our era—most notably, his early funding of Facebook—as well as his cultivation of a persona defined by elegance, detachment, and strategic brilliance. The film was satirical in its depiction of Thiel as a demigod. The irony, of course, was that none of his accomplishments were exaggerated. Thiel is the billionaire's billionaire, an architect of the systems that shape our digital and political world. Less visible than the public-facing figures he supports,

Thiel nonetheless exerts a subterranean, strategic influence, quietly setting the coordinates for the future others are still trying to predict. The homage also focused on his impeccable style and tastes, and although it poked fun at its larger-than-life depiction, nothing represented in the film was an exaggeration. The facts were accurate. Thiel was the epitome of the heretic as defined by the conference—the cultural catalyst of the early twenty-first century, both vilified and celebrated.

The scientist turned to look at me and asked, "Is this supposed to be a parody?"

"Probably," I said. "It's all true, though."

The depiction seemed to also scandalize, in small measure, the military official, who laughed and looked toward me a few times, eyes questioning.

It was no secret that some members of the Founders Fund had an interest in UFOs. I was acquainted with and had worked alongside a small cohort of scientists and researchers who had come to be known as the Invisible College—a name chosen by none other than J. Allen Hynek, the most iconic figure in UFO history. Before the 1970s, these scientists had to keep their identities secret to protect their careers. Members of this cohort speculated that people like Thiel might be interested in the technology behind UFOs and possibly even the rumored reverse engineering programs that had been whispered about for the past sixty years. If such programs did exist, I had inadvertently uncovered one of them in my first book on the subject. As I documented there, I was taken on a trip into the desert by a well-placed aeronautics employee who showed me what he claimed were pieces of nonhuman technology—stored under lock and key—which he claimed to study.

"His is an intellect of rare genius," Jacques Vallée had once said, referring to Thiel. I thought of Jacques as a rare genius, so I set my expectations accordingly. I was already familiar with Thiel through the news—particularly as a harsh critic of academia. Thiel's position is that, in general, academia stifles innovation and rewards conformity instead of teaching students the skills of innovation and creativity. He created the Thiel Fellowship in 2011 and offered funds to support young entrepreneurs and to encourage them to pursue innovative projects outside the traditional four-year undergraduate university system.

A COMMON INFLUENCE: DR. RENÉ GIRARD AND HIS THEORY OF HUMAN VIOLENCE

I was surprised to discover that Thiel, who holds an undergraduate degree in philosophy from Stanford University, had been a student of René Girard. According to Thiel, Girard's work and character left a profound mark on him. The same was true for me, and at roughly the same time. I first encountered Girard's thought as an undergraduate in a religious studies course at the University of California, Davis, in the mid-1990s. The course was remarkable not only for its subject matter, but for its format: It was one of the first in the UC system to experiment with the "new" technology of videoconferencing. Several professors from across the UC campuses cotaught the class, which culminated in a conference at UCLA.

Five professors in total guided us through the primary text—Girard's *Violence and the Sacred*. It was an instance where academia embraced innovation in both form and content: We were learning through an emerging technology while studying a scholar so provocative that his public lectures had, on occasion, drawn picket lines. My curiosity deepened when I realized that, apart from my small circle of professors, Girard was often dismissed by other academics because his theory was a metatheory of violence, something that was critiqued—yet he retained a full professorship at Stanford. These criticisms, it seemed, had done nothing to diminish his stature.

To pass the course, I had to master the specifics of Girard's theory linking violence and religion. My professors spoke of Girard with reverence. I sensed that Girard was not just an academic figure, but something more than that. In his book he confronts the persistence of human violence, arguing that it operates according to a predictable logic he called the *scapegoat mechanism*. He maintained that while violence may be inevitable, it has an antidote. However, the underlying pattern of violence was the focus of the class.

THE SCAPEGOAT MECHANISM AND RELIGION

Girard identified what he called the scapegoat mechanism: a process by which a community in crisis redirects its collective aggression onto a single individual or group. This victim—though innocent—is blamed for the crisis, expelled, and sometimes killed. This group act of violence temporarily restores unity and relieves tension within the group. Girard argued that this is not an occasional social malfunction, but a foundational structure of culture itself.[1] The term draws from the biblical ritual in Leviticus, in which a priest symbolically transfers the community's sins onto a goat and sends it into the wilderness. While the ritual does not require killing the animal, the goat most likely dies from exposure—foreshadowing the fate of countless mythic, religious, and historical scapegoats, whose deaths underpin the logic of human sacrifice.

To this insight Girard added his theory of mimetic desire: Human beings do not desire something independently but learn what they want by imitating others. Inherent in imitation is rivalry, as people compete for the same jobs, partners, status, or recognition. When desire converges on the same object, competition escalates into conflict. In Girard's view, this rivalry is not an accident of human behavior—it is the system. At the breaking point, societies unconsciously seek out a scapegoat to bear the blame of conflict, whose expulsion or death restores temporary peace. The group murder of the scapegoat acts as a way to bring about group solidarity. A common enemy is a uniting force.

Religion, Girard argued, emerged as a cultural technology for managing this recurring cycle of violence. Sacrificial rituals channeled collective aggression onto a victim designated by the community or by divine will. Once the scapegoat was sacrificed and peace restored, the very success of the act convinced the community of the victim's guilt. The killing was no longer seen as murder, but as a sacred necessity. In this way, Girard argued that religion emerged as a coping mechanism as well as a deception to alleviate guilt and to make the foundational murder seem sacred.

Here, Girard adapted a psychoanalytic insight from Sigmund Freud's book about religion, *Totem and Taboo*. Freud believed that religion emerged through guilt; he speculates that a band of sons kills their father, appropriates his power, and then deifies him because they feel guilty. Girard revises Freud's theory and proposes that early religion formed when a community murdered a scapegoat and then projected divine sanction onto the act. The god's "demand" for sacrifice allowed the community to see itself as innocent. In this way, religious rituals and myths concealed violence beneath the appearance of holiness.

When I first learned about Girard's theory, I was confused. Most people, including me at that time, assume that religion is something about transcendence and God, and they are not used to identifying it as a cultural development that performs a function. Girard was an academic first, and a convert to Christianity later. He was able to see religion in ways that practitioners do not. Also, if I hadn't already taken other classes that gave me concrete examples, I might have missed the meaning of Girard's theories completely. Thankfully, my other coursework provided numerous examples of Girard's theory.

I studied early Christianity and learned that it began as a Jewish movement in the first century, under the rule of the Roman Empire. At that time, Roman religion wasn't just "mythology" in the way we think of it today; their gods and goddesses were the focus of public ceremonies, sacrifices, and devotion. What we call Greek and Roman myth today was religion in the first century for Greek and Roman people.

This was especially true in the Roman arenas, like the Colosseum. When most modern people picture the gladiator games, they think of them as bloody entertainment. But for Romans, these events were deeply religious. The ceremonies often began with prayers to gods like Saturn, Jupiter, or Hercules. Roman historian Kathleen Coleman was one of the first scholars to push back against the idea that the games were simply events for entertainment and pleasure. She revealed that they were actually ritual sacrifices that sometimes involved animals, but often involved human beings.[2]

These public killings were often staged to reenact the myths of gods and heroes. Prisoners of war, slaves, and early Christians could be forced to play the part of a divine figure in their final moments. For example, the hero Hercules was said to have died by setting himself on fire. Coleman cites a Roman account describing how a condemned man was burned alive in the arena to recreate Hercules's death. This was not an isolated event—these kinds of mythic "performances" were common. And yet, the Romans didn't call them human sacrifices, even though they clearly were. Instead, they saw them as sacred acts that strengthened their bond with their gods.

Girard's theory helps explain this. Societies often deal with tension and conflict by finding a scapegoat, a person or group to blame for the problem. Then they eliminate them. This act temporarily brings peace, and the community convinces itself that the victim was guilty or that their death was necessary. In the Roman arena, this pattern was repeated over and over: The victim was killed, the crowd felt justified, and life went on. For Girard, this is the dark side of religion—it can disguise murder as holiness, allowing people to feel innocent while taking part in collective violence.

As I read Girard's book and listened to my professors, I began to understand why he might have stirred controversy in the university. His scapegoat mechanism was a universal theory—a "big answer" to the question of why humans are so violent to each other. I assumed other scholars would challenge him simply because academics tend to be skeptical of grand, all-encompassing explanations. But the real flash point wasn't his claim that the pattern was universal, *it was his proposed antidote.*

In secular universities, professors of religious studies don't advocate for a particular faith. Yet Girard argued that the clearest historical revelation of the antidote to the scapegoat mechanism was found in the Jewish scriptures, culminating in the Christian New Testament. It wasn't that he set out to prove Christianity right; rather, he discovered this violent pattern in human history, and his primary evidence happened to be the canonical texts of the Western tradition. That raises an intriguing question: If Girard had been working within another culture's sacred literature, would he have found the same pattern—and the same type of antidote—there, too?

MORAL EVOLUTION

Girard's theory of human violence is grounded in historical sources and suggests an evolutionary trajectory in culture. In his view, the later narratives of Judaism and Christianity actively challenged the inevitability of scapegoating and collective murder. This intrigued me, and my coursework gave me opportunities to test his hypothesis against other historical material. I found similar patterns in Roman-era sources—one in particular that Girard himself never mentioned.

When I teach early Christianity, I assign *The Passion of Perpetua and Felicity* (*Passio Perpetuae et Felicitatis*). Perpetua was a twenty-two-year-old North African Roman citizen from an elite family. She wrote part of the document about her murder. It is the earliest surviving first-person narrative of a Christian martyr—and of a Christian woman. Her youth, which is the age of my students, makes her story especially relevant to them.

In the late second century, Christianity was of questionable status in Rome. Christians refused to sacrifice to the gods and goddesses of the empire, a refusal that could be interpreted as treason. Perpetua was condemned to die in the arena at Carthage in 203 CE, one of many forced into elaborate ritualized executions. As Coleman notes, Roman authorities attempted to dress Perpetua and her fellow Christians as priests and priestesses of Saturn and Ceres—casting them as symbolic figures in a sacrificial drama. This would have made them both offerings to and stand-ins for the Roman gods, enacting the very scapegoat mechanism Girard described.

Perpetua, however, refused to do this. She and her companions accepted execution in imitation of Jesus, but rejected participation in the Roman religious spectacle. In Girard's terms, this defiance is part of the historical "antidote" to the scapegoat system: a refusal to let collective murder be rebranded as sacred ceremony, or as religion. At this point, for Girard, is the birth of religion as an act of transcendence.

For Girard, early Christian resistance to the games marked a cultural shift. The canonical literature of Judaism and Christianity began to undermine the idea that peace required scapegoating. He argued that where most ancient myths concealed the innocence of the victim and justified their murder, the Gospels reverse this. Jesus becomes the ultimate scapegoat. He was innocent, yet executed by the crowd and state. His innocence is made explicit in the texts.

Girard maintains that because Jesus is presented as both human and divine, his unjust execution exposes scapegoating as a deceit that has shaped human culture. Jewish and then Christian theology, in Girard's view, does not perpetuate Rome's sacrificial logic; it challenges and overturns it. This is why the Gospel story, for Girard, is not just another sacrificial myth, it is the moment the logic of sacrifice is called into question.

I remember attending a Catholic Mass while studying this material and noticing the stone altar. It reminded me of the story in the Hebrew Bible where Abraham prepares to sacrifice Isaac. At the last moment, an angel stops him. Girard saw this as an early textual break with the ritual of sacrifice, one in which the divine does not demand the victim's death. That same break, he believed, reaches its fullest form in the Christian Passion narratives, where the system itself is laid bare.

WHAT CAN WE DO? GIRARD ON PERSONAL SANCTITY

I had heard from my professors that René Girard, who had been agnostic, converted to Christianity through his research, particularly by exploring suffering in the works of Fyodor Dostoevsky. In his book *Resurrection from the Underground: Feodor Dostoevsky,* Girard delves into Dostoevsky's portrayal of the "underground"—a realm characterized by isolation, alienation, and resentment. He interprets the underground not just as a psychological state but as a spiritual and existential condition, arising from the dynamics of mimetic desire and rivalry.

Dostoevsky's characters are not engaged in the brutal human sacrifices of first-century Rome and are thus more relatable to modern people. Ensnared in cycles of suffering, torn between self-destructive passions and the longing for redemption, their struggles are marked by envy, pride, and despair, the very elements of mimetic desire. Yet, within this darkness, Dostoevsky presents the possibility of transformation through a radical break from the cycles of vengeance and rivalry.

For Girard, Dostoevsky's insight was that freedom is in reach for those who relinquish mimetic rivalries. Several of Dostoevsky's protagonists illustrate the power of humility and sacrifice in overcoming resentment, envy, and self-loathing. Girard saw in Dostoevsky not just a psychologist of human suffering, but a visionary who illuminated the path to redemption through a focus on something beyond the obvious cycle of retribution and envy. Perhaps it was through Dostoevsky's vision of human nature that Girard recognized the possibility that one could break free from the cycles of envy, resentment, and of despising other people.

I was a graduate student at the Jesuit School of Theology on "Holy Hill" in Berkeley, California, when I was able to attend an evening seminar Girard held on the Stanford campus. He was humble in his interactions with students and knowing several of them, they told me that he often said that once one recognized the structure of human violence and injustice, and the suffering it causes, one had an obligation to resist it.

Once I understood that Girard possibly lived in a way that corresponded to what he wrote about, I felt that I could perhaps do it, too. He imparted a hope that it was possible to transcend violent tendencies and the suffering caused by mimetic desire and envy. One of Girard's devoted students was Gil Bailey, who has written extensively on Girard's work. Bailey describes the impact of Girard's theory on people who took the time to understand it.

> I first met Girard many years ago when he came to my office in Sonoma to spend the day with a group of biblical scholars discussing the implications of his work for biblical exegesis. Girard began the day by speaking for an

hour or so about his work, which proved to be material enough to fuel the discussion for the rest of the day. The burden of Girard's interventions was more or less that the Gospel was the driving force in human history, gradually plunging the world into a choice between the truth revealed by Christ and apocalyptic violence. At the end of the day, one of the scholars, reeling from the sweeping implications of what he had heard, asked Girard what should be done in the face of such a challenge. To the best of my memory—I have recounted this story many times—René replied: "Our situation does not lend itself to being easily 'fixed.' We are each called to different tasks, but perhaps we should all begin by striving for *personal sanctity*."[3]

* * *

Back in Berkeley, my professors wanted to know what I had learned from René Girard. Curiously, these discussions took place behind closed doors and in hushed voices. My professors, apparently, thought that Girard's theory *was that controversial*. One of them had even prepared me for these discussions by offering a special course specifically focused on the works of theologian Hans Urs von Balthasar, a prominent Swiss theologian who influenced the former Popes John Paul II and Benedict XVI. Balthasar had also been intrigued by Girard's work and thought that mimetic rivalry and the scapegoat mechanism were inspired contributions to Christian theology. While Balthasar valued Girard's contributions, he also offered critical reflections. He questioned whether Girard's framework sufficiently accounted for the divine initiative in the drama of salvation, suggesting that Girard's human-centered focus might underemphasize the role of God's engagement in human history.

I lean toward agreement with Balthasar. The antidote to human violence will probably arrive as something beyond the actions of human beings, yet I also believe that Girard identifies a real, repeatable pattern of violence that pervades certain rituals and media and that too often dominates group dynamics. The problem with Girard's theory for my Jesuit professors was that it was too anthropological, as Girard posed it as a problem that would ultimately be solved by human beings. The professors did not look to human beings for the answer to the problem of human violence, what they called *evil*, but put their faith in a God who they believed intervenes in human history.

These were the days of my formative training in religious studies. Looking back, it seems impossible for me to view it as a coincidence that this was happening within the very place—Silicon Valley and the greater Bay Area—where the mechanisms Girard identified, mimetic desire and the process of identifying and banishing (or canceling) a scapegoat, were being encoded into the architecture of the emerging digital world, our world today.

These memories came back to me as I sat with my friends in anticipation of Peter Thiel's talk, "Antichrist."

2

APOCALYPSE

> Then he will say to those on his left, "Depart from me, you who are cursed, into the eternal fire prepared for the devil and his angels. For I was hungry and you gave me nothing to eat, I was thirsty and you gave me nothing to drink, I was a stranger and you did not invite me in, I needed clothes and you did not clothe me, I was sick and in prison and you did not look after me."
>
> —MATT. 25:41–42

As we waited in the velvet seats of the theater for the clapping to die down after the video homage to Thiel, I struck up a conversation with two women who, like us, had found seats at the periphery of the main stage. They were both postdoctoral students, the younger of the two studying at MIT.

"What do you do?" the younger one asked me.

"I teach and write about religion," I said.

Her brow furrowed slightly, eyes searching for context. Almost everyone at the conference worked in the technology sector. She seemed confused as to why I was there.

Before we could continue the conversation, Thiel took

the stage and sat across from his guest speaker, who was a Christian minister. They wore crisp white shirts. The stage was set up to look like the comfortable, informal living room of your neighbor's home.

As the talk began, the room settled into silent, palpable anticipation. Thiel, ever the deliberate thinker, leaned forward and posed some thoughts, which, from my memory, began as a series of questions. He reminded the audience that the greatest deceiver, *the Antichrist,* is not generally described as an obvious tyrant, but a leader who promises comfort and safety. Instead of focusing on crude dystopias or authoritarian nightmares, Thiel emphasized the history of the Antichrist's representation within the Western tradition. Much of it suggests that the Antichrist would be insidious, and would endeavor to build a civilization built not on coercion, but on a collective surrender, even a willing submission to a system that promises peace. In other words, the Antichrist would propose a society based on things most people agree on. Those people who would not assent to the common good of all would appear to be irrational and this would set them up as social pariahs.

Since at least the first century, there has been an ongoing dialogue about apocalypse and what it means. Has it already happened, is it on the horizon, is it a literary genre based on fear and oppression? These questions accompany interpretations of apocalypse. Early Christians, living under the shadow of Rome, often read the Book of Revelation as a veiled indictment of imperial power, with the figure of the Beast understood as Emperor Nero. For them, the apocalypse was not merely an otherworldly finale, but a coded political critique, a call to discern the moral character of present realities. Later Catholic tradition layered this with theological nuance, seeing apocalyptic imagery as both a spiritual warning and a liturgical vision of God's ultimate justice. Other Christian denominations have interpreted apocalypse literally and have provided specific dates for it. In the nineteenth century, the American Baptist preacher William Miller offered yet another lens on the apocalypse. Interpreting biblical prophecy through a historicist reading of Daniel and Revelation, Miller predicted that Christ would return between 1843 and 1844. Thousands of followers, later called Millerites, sold possessions, left farms, and gathered on hilltops in anticipation. When the expected date passed without event, the movement suffered what came to be known as the "Great Disappointment." This hasn't prevented others from fixing a date and time. Harold Camping predicted that the apocalypse would occur on May 21, 2011. Sadly, thousands of people believed him and lost their homes and life savings when they donated them to his cause. In some instances, parents gave Camping their children's college savings. Instances like these have tainted public dialogue about apocalypse. When Thiel embraced the subject, the dialogue enjoyed renewed public engagement.

Thiel cited biblical and literary characterizations of the Antichrist. Notable among the latter was Robert Hugh Benson's *Lord of the World*. Benson's novel, published in 1907, is set in the early twenty-first century, and it tells the story of a world where nationalism has disappeared and consequently the world is controlled by a single government. Religions are marginalized and secular humanism is the dominant ideology. The Antichrist figure in the novel emerges as a Christlike, charismatic figure who unifies the world by abolishing religions and uniting people under a globalized state government. Traditional Christianity, as well as all religion, is suppressed and the powerful global government offers peace and unity through technological progress, euthanasia, and relativism.

Lord of the World has been referenced by former Popes Benedict XVI and Francis. Italian Cardinal Giacomo Biffi praised the book as prophetic, and argued that Benson foresaw the loss of a religious worldview and spiritual interiority in favor of a "benevolent secularism." Through his example of *Lord of the World,* Thiel emphasized that true control is not imposed but embraced. The most effective deceptions, he suggests, are the ones that feel like progress, where people willingly exchange their agency for what they believe will bring security and harmony. Unlike the oppressive dystopias of Orwell (*1984*) or Huxley (*Brave New World*), the world Benson envisioned—and the one Thiel warned about—emerges not from conquest but from consensus. The Antichrist, in this framework, would not appear as a tyrant but as a peacemaker offering solutions so rational and appealing that resistance would seem irrational, even dangerous.

As the discussion came to a close, it was clear that Thiel sought to elevate eschatology—considerations of what is commonly known as the end times—from the realm of cliché and caricature into a space of serious political and philosophical reflection. He had been workshopping this talk, readying it for prime time. This had to be, in itself, a historical moment with respect to the discourse surrounding the Antichrist, which, for good or bad, had been carried out within local nondenominational churches and even stigmatized by many theologians in the mainstream Anglican and Catholic Churches.

A buzz of voices erupted after the talk as people scrambled out of the theater to go to lunch. Thiel's assessment appeared to be that the Antichrist could be a person, or it could be a system, but it was definitely an offer of comfort and conformity over the pain of genuine conflict that accompanies contemporary national states of affairs. Perhaps this global government was something like the World Economic Forum. I couldn't remember if anyone asked him that question, or if there were questions after the talk.

At lunch I thought about Thiel's talk. I did not disagree with his assessment of the antireligious sentiments of globalized culture. Instead, I was surprised that he didn't engage with what I found to be the most significant parts of Benson's work. Much of the book focuses on the erasure of the interior life of human beings, their spiritual sense.

In *Lord of the World*, global unification is achieved not through overt tyranny, but by way of seductive technologies that promise to solve humanity's most intractable problems. Volors—advanced flying machines—collapse space and erase cultural differences, creating a seamless global landscape. Hospitals of Euthanasia offer state-sanctioned mercy in the face of suffering and aging, framing death as an act of compassion rather than a spiritual threshold. The world is no longer governed by mystery or transcendence but by the clock, statistics, and progress. In this rationalized order, religion is increasingly seen as disruptive, tribal, and obsolete—an emotional relic of a past tied to the rhythms of sun and moon.[1] Thiel emphasized these aspects of the book.

However, what emerges most forcefully in the book is not simply political or technological transformation, but the near-total loss of a spiritual worldview. This thematic core, an interior desolation masked by exterior harmony, is the heart of Benson's warning. Spiritual impoverishment is arguably the novel's most haunting dimension. In Benson's book, he paints the twenty-first-century world as a society drowned out by distraction. Interior life, which includes contemplation, reflection, and silence, is replaced by rationalism, and it almost completely disappears. Those who keep it alive and see it as important are called "the supernaturalists."

In Benson's future world, silence and solitude are suspect and almost everyone in the novel has lost the capacity to feel spiritual realities, not because they hate God, but because they've been numbed to the existence of them. They are not aware that they have an interior life or a spiritual sense. The members of Benson's society lack interiority, and because of that they are easy to pacify. They are not aware that there is something more interesting about life because the domain of the spirit and its gifts has been erased entirely.

If I were to identify a possible Antichrist, I would look for something with the capacity not only to erase the knowledge of the spiritual sense and the interior life, but also to physically diminish—or even reconfigure—the human faculty that makes such awareness possible. In the classical Christian tradition, this faculty is not an abstract metaphor but is understood to reside within the human body. Thomas Aquinas, in his search for a "sense" by which human beings apprehend the sacred, treats this capacity as real. To sever or distort this faculty would not simply impair religious imagination; it would obstruct the very mode of human perception through which divine reality is encountered.

Christian theology suggests that the Antichrist's foremost weapon is deception and the ability to infect hearts and minds with envy, lust, and avarice—the very qualities historically associated with evil. Thiel's critique of soft totalitarianism is not wrong, but it is incomplete. The Satan of the New Testament is characterized as the father of lies, the great deceiver, and the one who powers the Antichrist. As René Girard revealed, the deception at the heart of mimetic rivalry and violence results in events like the savagery of the Roman Colosseum, where a human sacrifice is perpetrated by people who believe they are not murdering a human being, but offering a gift to a god. If I were to wager on an Antichrist today, I'd replace the soft totalitarian theory with one in which digital platforms built on the algorithms of mimetic violence, as Girard described it, are the primary contenders.

THE DIVISION OF THE FLOCK

I was surprised that Thiel had not elaborated on the potential for digital media, specifically social media, to occupy the role of the Antichrist. As a student of Girard, I would have thought that he would see the inherently mimetic nature of social media—a system designed to amplify imitation, rivalry, and escalation. The monetary potential of these platforms lay precisely in their ability to fuel mimetic desire, driving users to imitate influencers, adopt trends, and engage in digital competition at an unprecedented scale. This was, as Girard himself warned, the very nature of unchecked imitation, a feedback loop that accelerates until it spirals out of control.

Girard observed that human beings are driven by mimetic desire, our wants are not entirely our own, but modeled on the desires of others. This dynamic produces rivalry, cycles of envy, and, if left unchecked, violence. Girard identified a recurring process of human behavior. In the 1990s, behavioral scientists like B. J. Fogg sought to harness predictable patterns of human behavior for technological persuasion. His field, *captology* (Computers as Persuasive Technologies), offered a framework: Identify a motivation, lower the difficulty of the behavior, and introduce a timely trigger. Fogg's intention was most likely not to manipulate brain chemistry, but to engineer environments in which people would reliably act in predictable ways.

Once this framework migrated from academic theory into Silicon Valley's commercial machinery, it fused with a different body of knowledge that emphasized operant conditioning. Social media platforms and recommendation engines began to use variable rewards, endless scroll, and notifications to keep users in a constant loop of anticipation and gratification. Coding effective algorithms—that is, those that hooked users—revealed that chemicals like dopamine could optimize products; therefore, coders created platforms that engaged users' physiologies.

What Girard had described as a timeless human pattern

was now transcribed into code. In the hands of engineers, mimetic behavior became an explicit design principle: Algorithms were trained to detect and amplify the objects, trends, and opinions that triggered the most imitation. The platforms industrialized the scapegoat mechanism. Once digitized, mimetic desire could be modeled, predicted, and endlessly looped back into the system, ensuring that the most imitable and often the most polarizing content was rewarded with maximum visibility. This transformed a behavior pattern into a physical infrastructure. The result was a cultural engine in which the algorithms themselves became mimetic actors, learning from and intensifying the very conflicts they provoke.

The worst of the platforms enact a kind of *algorithmic violence*. Research studies on the brains of youth are unsettling. There is a correlation between social media use and adverse brain development. Neuroimaging research shows that extensive digital media use in early childhood is associated with reduced cortical thickness in brain regions critical for attention, memory, letter recognition, and social cognition.[2] Social cognition includes the ability to feel empathy for others. Another study revealed that greater screen use predicted slower growth in global cortical surface area over time, suggesting long-term structural impacts on brain development.[3] Moving into adolescence, another study discovered that habitual social media checking heightened neural sensitivity in reward-related areas of the brain compared to peers who checked their phones less frequently.[4] Youth are particularly vulnerable due to the rapid development of their brains.

Each of the studies note that there is a significant impact

on social cognition, foremost being empathy. Significantly, social cognition roughly corresponds to those faculties that compose the interior life. They include feeling what others might be feeling; understanding what they feel; and judging fairness, truthfulness, and moral responsibility. This form of erosion of the interior life is even worse than that described in Benson's novel, as this is a developmental stage in human maturity, and once it is over, the chance of regaining these traits is small. At least in Benson's novel the spiritual faculties are still intact. They are just forgotten. In today's climate, they are at risk for deletion.

Who will be the modern versions of Perpetua, the young woman who stood up to the Roman death machinery and refused to participate in and feed its continuation? They are few in number, but there are people who intuitively resist the digital iteration of the scapegoat mechanism. On the other hand, I have also met people who have been a part of the teams who have coded the platforms. I had a memorable conversation with one of them who was well aware of the changes that these products would wreak.

"There will be a bifurcation, globally. The division will happen through the use of AI-powered social media. The division will be between those who use the technology critically and do not lose their lives to it; they will enjoy the outdoors, the gifts of the outside world. Those who unthinkingly use it will eventually be ruled by it. The former limit their screen time," they said.

"Do not live your life online. You will lose your life, like millions of others. Instead, go outside, enjoy the grass, the trees, the fresh air. And teach your children to do this, too," they warned.

Whatever the case, the situation is that algorithmic feedback technologies have a specific influence on human physiology, which in some cases is good, and in many cases is not.

Months before I attended Hereticon, I spoke at a Catholic school whose rhythms are still ordered by prayer and contemplation. Here, in a place designed to preserve and pass along the interior life, the question was not whether algorithms were shaping human desires—it was how to resist them without becoming cultural exiles. The audience was a mixture of academics, elementary and high school teachers, parents, monks, priests, and sisters, a variety of people whose common concern was the preservation of empathy, goodness, and qualities that make life worth living. My talk focused on the vulnerability of youth and I related studies about the neurological impacts of social media, being careful to note that these are correlations and that causality has not been proven.

When the group broke for lunch, I was surrounded by teachers whose faces wore the same expression: sealed mouths and set jaws. They appeared resigned and grim.

"We need to talk with you," one of them said.

"In our schools the kids use their phones. We cannot take them. Almost weekly a group of kids will single one child out and they will all gang up on and bully that child using their phones, using social media. The bullied children are sometimes suicidal."

In my talk, I hadn't discussed Girard's theory of the

scapegoat mechanism, but here it was being linked to social media by these teachers. They looked like sad soldiers, battle weary from the front.

"This is terrible, I'm so sorry you're dealing with this," I said.

"We are all dealing with this," another woman said.

They all nodded their heads.

"Can you take the phones from them?" I asked. It seemed unbelievable to me that schools allow students to have their phones in the classroom.

"No."

"Have you talked to their parents?" I asked. I know that there are parents who do not allow their children to have phones until they reach a certain age.

"The parents are on their phones, too," said the teacher who originally spoke up. "They are as bad as their kids."

She continued to express her frustration, and again, unknowingly, she linked it back to Girardian theory.

"The kids, and their parents, when I explain how this makes the bullied child feel, it is like they don't understand. I've tried so many ways to explain this, but their faces go blank. They do not understand. It is more than not having empathy," she said. "It's like they don't even know it exists. And there are lots of them, not just one or two. I've been teaching for thirty years, and this is different," she said.

We all stood in silence. There was a feeling of sadness, resignation, and even fear among the small group.

"You think it is worse than not having empathy?" I asked.

She nodded yes.

"It no longer exists in their minds, or something," she said.

Utilizing the Catholic and Christian records and their visionary literature, Thiel warned that a certain type of global government fits the historical definition of the Antichrist—a central authority that seduces the world with promises of order and security. Yet, here is a diffuse, invisible network shaping human behavior at scale—without overt coercion. What the teachers described to me was precisely this: a decentralized digital infrastructure that bypasses political authority, yet penetrates the most intimate spaces of childhood. Algorithms that exploit the scapegoat mechanism do not seize power through force; they enfold users, imperceptibly, within their logic. This is not a government. By its nature it is dispersed, and nearly inescapable. If an Antichrist exists, and theologically that is up for debate, I'd wager it was the specific technological environments identified by those teachers, systems that quietly dismantle the interior life, eroding the very neural and spiritual foundations of empathy and other senses that open a human being to wonder and the sacred.

Girard recognized that human evil often follows a patterned sequence, recursive, self-reinforcing, and, in a sense, algorithmic. His work, like that of other Catholic visionaries examined here, remained on the periphery of the institutional church. Pierre Teilhard de Chardin, the Jesuit priest and paleontologist, was likewise sidelined; his writings were banned for decades, dismissed or misunderstood. Yet both men intuited forces whose outlines have become startlingly clear in our century. What they glimpsed, like the automation of desire, the mechanization of the sacred, and the quiet erasure of interiority, is no longer speculative. It is embedded in our devices, and, as the teachers' stories attest, it is reshaping the human person from the inside out.

THE HERETICS OF SPIRITUAL EVOLUTION: MARGINALIZED CATHOLIC VISIONARIES

The premise of Hereticon—that cultural revolutionaries are rarely recognized in their time and often and at best marginalized or ignored—applies to a small cohort of Catholic visionaries who predicted a world so strange that it rivals science fiction. Their predictions don't look like a globalized and spiritually bereft secular humanism. They are also unlike any of the well-known and widely read dystopias like Aldous Huxley's *Brave New World* or George Orwell's *1984*. These are tame and normal in comparison. Instead, they resemble Arthur C. Clarke's science fiction horror story, *Childhood's End*, which describes how the children of Earth are subsumed into an alien network called the Overmind. It's little wonder the church hierarchy ignored them at the time; they had no frame of reference for what these visionaries described. Now, in the early twenty-first century as the world is confronted with new forms of technological intelligence, their visions appear prophetic.

3

THE APOCALYPTIC EVENT

> No civilian can escape this environmental blitzkrieg, for there is, quite literally, no place to hide.
>
> —MARSHALL MCLUHAN, "THE *PLAYBOY* INTERVIEW"

I return to Miami to visit Vince Gerardis, who is best known as the co-executive producer of *Game of Thrones*. He offers me a fizzy water as we look out the wide glass wall of his studio, which faces the Atlantic Ocean. The water is deep blue, and after a while, a soft fog rolls in like slow-moving tumbleweeds made of mist—light gray, weightless, and so perfectly timed it feels scripted.

Vince is an almost introverted person who practices a Californian, New Age form of spirituality. He endeavors to treat people with dignity, and not as a means to an end. Even though we share that value, the world he inhabits is far removed from my own. He spends his time making deals related to the movie and television industry.

"The view is never the same," Vince says as we gaze out the window. The ocean view pulls me in, and I am mesmerized. Vince's studio is many stories off the ground. I feel like I'm sitting on the clouds looking down into the water. The color blue fills the room, from the sky view to the color of Vince's eyes, which are laser focused on the churning waves.

Vince thinks this is a business meeting, but I remember it as the day I discovered that the novel *Childhood's End* is prophecy disguised as science fiction. Vince is known to bring speculative worlds to the screen, and his instincts are good. *A Game of Thrones*, for example, was a book he championed before fantasy had reentered the cultural mainstream. Science fiction, which often predicts future technological developments with some accuracy, is sometimes referred to as a secular prophetic tradition. If that's the case, then Vince, knowingly or not, has been one of its most accurate readers.

"The classic, of course, is *Childhood's End*," he says. "Everything is in that book."

Before the meeting, I remembered the book as a fun read and an engaging alien invasion narrative that was better than most. After the meeting, I saw it as a road map for the contemporary digital era.[1] The novel's plot involves the split of the human race by generation: children and adults. The children are abducted by an intelligent network called the Overmind. The abduction is abetted by extraterrestrials who look exactly like biblical demons. There, in Vince's studio, as I watched the ocean waves lap the pale sand of the Miami shore, I "got" the book.

I returned home and reread it. It is partially a reinterpretation of traditional religion as contact with extraterrestrials. Perhaps the novel is the first well-known media to make this move, as this reinterpretation takes many forms in contemporary culture. The classic example of this revision is the television series *Ancient Aliens*, as it reinterprets contact with the gods as being contact with aliens, popularly known as the ancient astronaut theory. *Childhood's End* is a different version of this, as the alien is an extraterrestrial "network." The novel also portrays mysticism, defined as being direct knowledge of the sacred, as being a misinterpretation. In the novel, mysticism and contact with God are recast as attempts by an alien species to make contact with human beings. Arthur C. Clarke's characterization of the alien species as a network is more in line with contemporary digital technology than that of *Ancient Aliens*. If there were, as some popular ufologists claim, an actual alien agenda, it would be, as Vince said, all there in that book, *Childhood's End*.

SCIENCE FICTION AS SECULAR PROPHETIC LITERATURE

Could science fiction be a prophetic tradition of secular culture? From the second half of the twentieth century, a group of scholars emerged whose work grappled with the unusually predictive aspects of science fiction. In his book *Eros and Magic in the Renaissance*,[2] Ioan Couliano argued that science fiction, much like Renaissance magic, enables individuals to explore and influence the trajectory of human knowledge and societal evolution. Science fiction, he argued, is a continuation of religion and works alongside it as a form of modern mythmaking, using symbols and mythology to convey information about the future. He also credited science fiction with the production of real social effects. Jeffrey Kripal, a younger contemporary of Couliano, argues that science fiction not only reflects current scientific understanding, but also anticipates future developments, effectively serving as a predictive tool for cultural and scientific evolution.[3]

These scholars not only attend to the interplay between imagination, cultural narratives, and the shaping of human consciousness and culture, but they also explore how speculative and creative expressions, such as science fiction, transcend storytelling to become tools for viewing and even influencing future possibilities. By examining the mechanisms through which imagination interacts with societal structures, they highlight the power of symbols, myths, and creative works to act as forces for cultural change and progress.

While it is perhaps controversial to elaborate on predictive capacities within a genre of literature like science fiction, it is not controversial to write about prophecy in religious traditions. Prophecy is generally defined as a genre of oral tradition and literature distinguished by its predictive character. Couliano maintained that science fiction works like prophecy in modern times in that it predicts and even shapes the future.

Examples of science fiction that have predicted real technologies abound. Jules Verne, in *Twenty Thousand Leagues Under the Sea* (1870), famously predicted and inspired a sea vehicle that would become the submarine approximately one hundred years later. His *Nautilus* was powered by electricity, had a pressurized hull, and a navigation system. In his *From the Earth to the Moon* (1865), Verne also predicted that the rocket and spacecraft would launch from Florida, near Cape Canaveral. Mary Shelley's *Frankenstein; Or, the Modern Prometheus*, widely regarded as the first work of science fiction, not only predicted genetic engineering, organ transplantation, and synthetic biology, but most significantly, she predicted the ethical and moral issues accompanying the use of such technologies.

Scholars Patrick Parrinder and James McGrath have also explored the predictive qualities of science fiction and draw comparisons with prophecy. Parrinder differentiates science fiction from traditional prophecy by arguing that, rather than delivering divine or authoritative predictions, science fiction relies on the use of myth and symbols to explore abstract ideas and philosophical questions, offering meaning through storytelling rather than doctrinal certainty.[4] Similarly, McGrath examines science fiction's predictive nature and its parallels with prophecy.[5] However, both scholars ultimately view science fiction and prophecy as cultural narratives—stories that societies create to make sense of their lives and the cosmos. In their analyses, these genres are reduced to tools for cultural self-reflection rather than vehicles for actual predictions.

According to Couliano and Kripal, there is more to science fiction than being just explanatory stories. Couliano argues that both prophecy and science fiction function as tools for shaping reality.[6] They argue that science fiction does not merely reflect cultural narratives, but actively influences human knowledge and societal evolution by enabling people to envision alternate future possibilities. Imagination has a tangible effect on the world, blurring the line between mythmaking and reality. Kripal reveals that science fiction operates as a future-focused mysticism, capable of both reflecting current scientific understanding and inspiring leaps into uncharted realms of thought. Science fiction catalyzes cultural and scientific breakthroughs.[7] These scholars offer a way of understanding science fiction as not just modern myth, but as a channel through which humanity taps into latent knowledge, including knowledge of the future.

Arthur C. Clarke understood science fiction in much the same way that Couliano and Kripal did, but much earlier. As Clarke beat the keys of his typewriter and penned his notes for his books and essays, he believed that science fiction did more than predict the future—it helped create it. Clarke was very aware and proud of his work that predicted and helped create real future space technology. In an early essay, "Extra-Terrestrial Relays: Can Rocket Stations Give World-wide Radio Coverage?" (1945), Clarke proposed placing three satellites in geostationary orbit—that is, positioning a satellite above a specific place on Earth, in order to provide global radio coverage.[8] This idea eventually inspired engineers to develop satellites called Telstar (1962). The geostationary orbit is informally referred to as the "Clarke Orbit" in his honor.[9]

Clarke is best known for his collaboration with movie producer Stanley Kubrick on *2001: A Space Odyssey* (1968). Uniquely, the book and film were conceived together, with

Clarke developing the philosophical framework and narrative, while Kubrick shaped the cinematic language. The result was not merely a story about space exploration, but a meditation on the evolution of consciousness, the future of artificial intelligence, and humanity's place within a vast, mostly silent cosmos. HAL 9000, the sentient-like computer, prefigures the ethical dilemmas of AI, including its capacity to murder human beings. The film's iconic black monolith, which looks like a large modern smartphone, functions in the film like an alien intelligence, triggering human development while remaining mysterious and inscrutable. In both the film and novel, artificial and extraterrestrial intelligences converge at a pivotal moment in human evolution. Are they connected in some way that is not obvious, or that is obvious in retrospect?

Clarke's first published book was nonfiction—*Interplanetary Flight: An Introduction to Astronautics* (1950). It is a work of popular science that helped shape the public understanding of space exploration in the pre–space age. The book covers the fundamental physics of rocket propulsion and orbital mechanics, making Newtonian laws accessible to a general audience. It also describes the challenges of spacecraft design, from propulsion systems to structural concerns, and outlines the practical possibilities of reaching the moon and planets beyond.

Clarke was a member of the British Interplanetary Society (BIS), founded in 1933, which was one of the first institutions in the world to treat the idea of space travel not as fantasy, but as a legitimate area of scientific and technical exploration. Long before Sputnik or NASA, the BIS served as an imagination laboratory, where scientists, engineers, and writers came together to envision the future of humanity beyond Earth. Clarke's satellite idea was germinated within this think tank and later published as a BIS publication. For Clarke, and for many within the BIS, imagination was integral to applied science. The society's speculative projects—like Project Daedalus, a conceptual interstellar spacecraft using nuclear fusion, or their early crewed Lunar Spaceship design from 1939—anticipated real-world space missions by decades. The BIS was a haven for writers who would go on to define modern science fiction, such as Clarke and, later, Stephen Baxter, author of the NASA Trilogy. For them, the "impossible" was simply the not-yet-engineered. Clarke and his colleagues understood science fiction as narrative architecture of the future.

CHILDHOOD'S END MEETS THE MEDIA THEORIES OF MARSHALL McLUHAN

Childhood's End is eerily resonant with the technological and metaphysical concerns of the 2020s. If science fiction is a form of future architecture, then Clarke drafted blueprints for a transformation far deeper than the arrival of any single device: the transformation of human consciousness itself.

Though writing fiction in the 1950s, Clarke's concerns closely parallel those of Canadian media theorist Marshall McLuhan, whose nonfiction writing in the 1960s explores the effects of media on perception, cognition, and human consciousness. Where Clarke tells the story of a species-wide metamorphosis catalyzed by alien intelligence, McLuhan charts the slow, imperceptible rewiring of human beings by the very tools we invent. Together, Clarke and McLuhan sketch the outlines of a new kind of being emerging from an environment that McLuhan called *supraterrestrial*.

McLuhan's signature insights—"the medium is the message," "the global village," and "the extensions of man"—are more than clever turns of phrase.[10] For him, media are not passive conveyors of content but active agents of change. Each medium extends the human nervous system, and in doing so, reorganizes the structures of consciousness. The printing press made linear, individual thought possible; electric media collapsed time and space, creating a tribalized, collective sensibility. When we create new technologies, we often think of them as tools that make our lives easier or more powerful. McLuhan said these tools are actually "extensions" of our bodies and minds. For example, a car is an extension of our feet, and a smartphone is an extension of our brain. But McLuhan also warned that every time we extend ourselves through technology, we lose something, too. We stop using the part of ourselves that the tool replaces. Over time, this can make us less thoughtful, less aware of our inner feelings, and more focused on what's happening outside us. He believed that the more we depend on screens and machines, the harder it becomes to have an inner life filled with reflection, imagination, and silence. McLuhan argues that interior life becomes externalized.[11]

Clarke dramatizes this transformation in *Childhood's End*, where an alien species presides over the final dissolution of human individuality. In the novel, children are absorbed into a collective intelligence that functions like a hive mind, and they cease to be recognizably human. Read through McLuhan's lens, this is not just a tale of alien contact, but a prophetic meditation on the end of the modern subject and the emergence of a new form of consciousness.

While Clarke's hybrid humans—the children abducted by the Overmind—would be a devastating development, it is portrayed as fiction. The supraterrestrial found in the works of Catholic visionaries like Pierre Teilhard de Chardin, Marshall McLuhan, and others is a theological prediction that remains, for them, hopefully optimistic. As they see it, the supraterrestrial is an evolutionary intensification of spiritual consciousness. Clarke, by contrast, envisions an intelligence that invades and supplants the human, with no clear room for the redemption of the human being. Where the visionaries see hope, Clarke depicts the end, or evolution, of the human being.

McLUHAN'S SUPRATERRESTRIAL—THE ALIEN IS US

McLuhan's first use of the term *supraterrestrial* is from a 1969 interview in *Playboy* magazine.[12] He coined it while exploring the idea that media function as extensions of the human nervous system. As technology accelerates, he argued, it draws humanity beyond its biological limits. The supraterrestrial, for McLuhan, is not a space traveler from another planet, but a new human being—one shaped by global media systems, disembodied perception, and the collapse of traditional spatial and temporal boundaries.

The term appears in the context of his discussion of media as extensions of the human nervous system and his increasing concern with the psychological and spiritual consequences of technological environments. By *supraterrestrial*, McLuhan meant a condition in which humanity, through electronic media and space-age technologies, begins to exist beyond the limitations of the earthbound body and environment. It is not merely a reference to outer space or extraterrestrials, but to a new way of being human, perhaps *Homo sapiens'* evolutionary successor.

The supraterrestrial human is no longer defined by biological or local constraints, but by connectivity, simultaneity, and the integration of consciousness across the globe. Satellites, radio, and television—what McLuhan called "electronic media"—produce a planetary nervous system. The body is extended and abstracted, and what results is a new ontological condition: the human as supraterrestrial, mediated and disembodied. He viewed this as both exhilarating and catastrophic, a kind of technological apotheosis—a transformation of the species that parallels the prophecies of mystical traditions.

McLuhan was a Catholic convert and embedded within the Catholic theological tradition. He was simultaneously hopeful and suspicious of the arrival of the supraterrestrial. On the one hand, throughout the 1950s and '60s he observed its nascent effects and the potential catastrophe it might wreak upon human culture. On the other hand, he identified a stream of hope within the Catholic prophetic tradition, as far back as Dante Alighieri. Elaborating on this point, McLuhan states:

"Psychic communal integration, made possible at last by the electronic media, could create the universality of consciousness foreseen by Dante when he predicted that men would continue as no more than broken fragments until they were unified into an inclusive consciousness. This is a new interpretation of the mystical body of Christ; and Christ, after all, is the ultimate extension of man."[13]

By invoking Dante's concept of unity, McLuhan positions modern media as a fulfillment of that prophetic vision, where humanity transcends individual fragmentation to achieve a holistic consciousness. This is the networked self in its most hopeful interpretation. Dante wrote about the human body transfigured by the vision of God. His use of the term *trasumanar*, which translates as, "to transhumanize," is the first use of the term *transhuman*. Dante explicitly treats this process as being initiated by the divine, by the beatific vision, a process through which a good person—in Dante's case this was his love, Beatrice—is transformed into a divine version of a human being.[14]

In *Childhood's End*, Clarke offers a darker version of *Homo sapiens'* successor. Where McLuhan imagines the supraterrestrial as an emergent state of humanity—an extension of the human collective consciousness brought about by the intensification of media—Clarke presents it as a wholly other intelligence. In *Childhood's End*, the supraterrestrial arrives not from within human culture but from beyond it, in the form of an alien species whose purpose is to shepherd humanity into a final evolutionary surrender. This is not integration, but obliteration. While McLuhan holds out hope that media might fulfill a Christian eschatology, or end-time view, of union through Christ—the ultimate extension of the human being—Clarke offers an end-time view of extinction. His Overlords and the Overmind are not extensions of human potential, but alien powers that render humanity obsolete. In this way, Clarke's vision of the supraterrestrial is antihuman: a transformation that comes not as fulfillment, but as erasure.

In the next chapter, I turn to *Childhood's End* as a vessel for McLuhan's supraterrestrial logic and a modern reimagining of the Antichrist narrative. Where earlier visions like *Lord of the World* warned of totalitarianism cloaked by the facade of spiritual peace, Clarke offers a subtler prophecy: the dissolution of the self through the seduction of progress. His novel presents a future already taking shape—one in which privacy disappears, individuality fades, and the children of the world are absorbed into a collective, networked mind. This transformation arrives not with brute force, but through the guidance of extraterrestrials who look like classical demons yet act with dispassionate reason and offer helpful technologies.

Significantly, the novel replaces traditional religion with something modern people might find more realistic than the God of the past: extraterrestrials who appear to help human beings on their evolutionary path. The initial critical receptions of the novel lauded its conclusions as a tragic yet rational and therefore mature inevitability, subject to evolutionary determinism, where religion is represented as archaic and old-fashioned. Clarke's vision offers a stark invitation: to consider whether our surrender to the networked world is not salvation, but transfiguration of a more perilous kind.

4

THE CHILD NETWORK

> The barriers of distance are crumbling; one day we shall meet our equals, or our masters, among the stars.
>
> —ARTHUR C. CLARKE, FOREWORD TO *2001: A SPACE ODYSSEY*

If *Lord of the World* envisions the suppression of religion and the interior life through global secularism, *Childhood's End* suggests the same endgame, but through different means: the replacement of religion through technology provided by an alien species. Rather than depicting religion under siege, Clarke shows it being outmoded—not eradicated by force, but rendered obsolete by a rationalism reinforced through propaganda machines.

In this sense, *Childhood's End* aligns with the Antichrist narrative of deception wherein even the best of us is fooled. It does not warn of an external tyranny; it reveals the inward colonization of spiritual intuition. Where *Lord of the World* stages a conflict between belief and unbelief, or the supernaturalists and the rationalists, Clarke's novel stages a future in which belief is no longer necessary because the very thing that once required belief—the recognition of a spiritual connection to the sacred—is reinterpreted and replaced with a connection to an alien network. Interiority to the sacred disappears and is supplanted by a direct connection to the alien species.

Childhood's End begins with the global sighting of alien spaceships arriving in the skies over the major cities of Earth. Soon after, a single representative from the spaceships, Karellen, communicates with Earthlings. Karellen declares that they will help humans resolve long-standing problems such as scarcity, war, and pollution. Karellen is an "Overlord," a seemingly beneficent emissary of a consciousness called the Overmind. While remaining hidden in their spaceships, the Overlords act as stewards who help humans usher in a new, utopian world, a golden age of humanity. However, it is quite unnerving to humans when, after fifty years, the Overlords reveal their appearance. They are winged beings with horns, red scaly skin, and tails—no less than the Christian depiction of demons. Soon after this revelation of the Overlords' appearance, human children begin to display telepathic abilities and a psychic connection with each other and with the Overmind—the entity that appears to orchestrate this transformation. They act in unison as if they share one mind. The children become alienated from their parents and from worldly and earthly connections as they merge with the Overmind. This signals, as Clarke's title implies, not just the end of childhood as a metaphor, but the end of a stage in human evolution defined by individuality, familial bonds, and traditional religion. It also ends *Homo sapiens*. Do the children embody the promised next stage in human evolution, as the Overlords insist—or are they evidence of a colonization, a subsuming of humanity by a nonhuman intelligence whose motives are ultimately hostile?

Since its publication, *Childhood's End* has received a favorable literary reception and is widely regarded as a classic in science fiction literature. It presents humanity's transition to the Overmind as both inevitable and tragic—a necessary step in human evolution. In the story, the Overlords, despite being literal demons in appearance—are portrayed as being midwives of human evolution. The archetype of the demonic is reimagined in Karellen, the Overlords' leader, as a kindly but imposing figure akin to an older, wiser friend or uncle. Recent interpretations of the book are less clear about the novel's outcome.

Readings of the novel that interpret it as being predictive of the internet and artificial intelligence are relatively recent, emerging primarily in the twenty-first century as these technologies became more prominent. As media scholar Marshall McLuhan wrote, new technology constitutes a new human "environment."[1] In McLuhan's terms, an environment is not just a backdrop, but an active force—something that reshapes how we think, feel, and relate to others without our full awareness. What was seen as a helpful revelation in the earlier interpretations of the book—that human fears of technological progress are naive—is reexamined in light of contemporary technological developments. Through the lens of current events, the Overlords are not benign. Instead, they are demons in the traditional meaning of that word; they are agents of destruction.

TECHNOLOGICAL SATURATION AND THE SUPRATERRESTRIAL

McLuhan's theories illuminate Clarke's vision and its themes of technology's effects on consciousness. His unique insight was that the content of media was secondary to the form and structure of media itself—that is, the materiality of media is what mattered most. The effect of technology media on human beings and culture does not lie in what it says or means, but rather in how screens, instantaneous connectivity, and computer algorithms shape human cognition and physiology, and thus impact culture in unexpected ways. He noted that while this has always been the case with technological development, the advent of digital technology would disrupt and shift human society and human beings in ways that rival the invention of writing itself, and the printing press. He argued that the increasingly technological environment would inaugurate a new type of human being and culture and punctuated this shift with reference to generational shifts: "The generation gap is actually a chasm, separating not two age groups but two vastly divergent cultures."[2]

McLuhan predicted that the nature of this new environment would be all-encompassing and impervious to most, if not all, attempts to mediate it.

> Our whole cultural habitat, which we once viewed as a mere container of people, is being transformed by these media and by space satellites into a living organism, itself contained within a new macrocosm or connubium of a supraterrestrial nature.[3]

He clarifies this point:

> This is the real use of the computer, not to expedite marketing or solve technical problems but to speed the process of discovery and orchestrate terrestrial—and eventually galactic—environments and energies. Psychic communal integration, made possible at last by the electronic media, could create the universality of consciousness foreseen by Dante when he predicted that men would continue as no more than broken fragments until they were unified into an inclusive consciousness.[4]

McLuhan's notion of the supraterrestrial helps us understand the *Childhood's End* map of the imagined future.

THE APOCALYPTIC MOMENT: WHAT IS COMING

While McLuhan anticipated this transformation through media, Clarke dramatized its unfolding in human society through suspense and silence. Most of the action of *Childhood's End* involves waiting. After the arrival of the spaceships, human beings from all governments wait for the Overlords to reveal themselves. Karellen relates that this period will take fifty years. Once that time passes and Karellen reveals himself, another waiting period will begin. While Karellen is optimistic about what they are waiting for, humans are not yet convinced that they should look forward to this imminent event. However, the time spent between the revelation of Karellen's appearance and the end point he insists is coming is referred to as "the Golden Age." Most diseases and problems, including world hunger and poverty, are abolished by the superior technology of the Overlords, and human beings finally live together peacefully and enjoy longevity and happiness. Clarke notes that, at this point and for the most part, "No one worried but a few philosophers."[5]

The philosophically minded are suspicious of the remaking of human culture. They decide to band together and live on an island they name "New Athens." They want it to be a sanctuary for preserving what makes human beings unique. They safeguard the pursuit of art created not for profit, but for its own sake, inquiry driven by curiosity rather than utility, and the bonds between parents and children. Central to their vision is the preservation of human community—defined as person-to-person interaction through physical presence. An inhabitant of New Athens says, "Here in Athens, entertainment takes its proper place. Moreover, it's live, not canned. In a community this size it is possible to have complete audience participation with all that that means to the performers and artists."[6] The same character noted with horror that, in the world outside New Athens, "the average viewing time per person is now three hours a day. Soon people won't be living their own lives anymore."[7]

While most people in the world enjoy the fruits of the gifts of the Overlords, the suspense of what is coming disturbs the minds of those who pause long enough between their leisurely activities to consider it. Nobody can actually say what it is that's coming, but there are indications that it will be *definitive*. For one thing, it will not be stopped or abated by any human-made system, like governments. Clarke writes, "The Overlords seemed largely indifferent to forms of government, provided that they were not oppressive or corrupt."[8] Apparently, what is coming is unprecedented, and the indifference of the Overlords to any governmental system suggests that the organized efforts of human beings, such as those found in governments or revolutionary movements, will be irrelevant. The power of *what is coming* will be greater than the power of political institutions and governments. In Benson's *Lord of the World*, the power of the Antichrist is characterized in similar ways. His power is not institutional, nor can institutions stop him. In chapter 6, we will explore Mark Stahlman's argument that nations, governments, and political systems are powerless to stop the encroachment of what he calls the Digital Sphere.

McLuhan's characterization of the coming age of AI and technologies of connection is similar. He often states that human beings will be completely unprepared for AI's disruption. In 1969, he said, "If you have difficulty envisioning something as trivial as the imminent end of elections, you'll be totally unprepared to cope with the prospect of the forthcoming demise of spoken language and its replacement by a global consciousness."[9] Elections, the epitome of modern human agency, in both Clarke's view and in McLuhan's description of the future, will be irrelevant. So, too, will privacy.

SOCIAL ENGINEERING AND SURVEILLANCE: THE END OF COGNITIVE SOVEREIGNTY

During the fifty-year time frame in which humans wait for the Overlords to reveal their appearance, religions are deemed to be superstitions based on lies. "Fifty years is ample time in which to change a world and its people almost beyond recognition."[10] This shift is brought about through Karellen's use of social engineering.

Social engineering was a term that was, in part, made famous by author Aldous Huxley. In his dystopian novel *Brave New World*, he characterizes it as a comprehensive system of education and propaganda that his dystopic world, the World State, uses to control its population. Huxley spoke publicly about the use of social engineering by governments to pacify its populations, to control not through force, but through manipulation and seduction. He noted that this form of control was more effective than force, as people would enjoy and welcome their servitude, instead of resisting it.[11] Clarke's Overlords in *Childhood's End* operate on the same principle: They guide and constrain humanity by engineering consent, shaping culture, education, and incentives, rather than ruling through terror.

The Overlords provide human beings with a remote viewing technology that allows them to view any place at any time in the past. Among other historical events, people view the lives of religious founders like the Buddha and Jesus Christ. Once people allegedly see the actual circumstances of the lives of these men, within a generation almost everyone on Earth loses their faith. The miracles associated with each were either not viewable through the technology, or, they never happened. People assumed the miracles never happened. The question of whether the technology was accurate or controlled is never addressed by the characters.

Karellen's social engineering also has the effect of shifting the long-held association of the image of the classical demon with evil. When Karellen finally unveils himself by stepping out of his spaceship he looks like a stereotypical demon. "There was no mistake. The leathery wings, the little horns, the barbed tail—all were there. The most terrible of all legends had come to life, out of the unknown past."[12] Yet, as Clarke writes, most people had already lost their fear of the Overlords, and there were only a few left who recognized their association with demons. "It was a tribute to the Overlords' psychology, and to their careful years of preparation, that only a few people fainted."[13] The efforts of the Overlords to rebrand themselves within fifty years worked. The few people who associated the Overlords with historical demons were thought to be superstitious and old-fashioned.

In Clarke's and McLuhan's work, social engineering is assumed to be of service to an evolutionarily beneficial goal. McLuhan lauds the computer's utopic possibilities:

> The computer can be used to direct a network of global thermostats to pattern life in ways that will optimize human awareness. Already, it's technologically feasible to employ the computer to program societies in beneficial ways. There's nothing at all difficult about putting computers in the position where they will be able to conduct carefully

> orchestrated programming of the sensory life of whole populations. I know it sounds rather science-fictional, but if you understood cybernetics you'd realize we could do it today.
>
> We could program five hours less of TV in Italy to promote the reading of newspapers during an election, or lay on an additional 25 hours of TV in Venezuela to cool down the tribal temperature raised by radio the preceding month. By such orchestrated interplay of all media, whole cultures could now be programed in order to improve and stabilize their emotional climate, just as we are beginning to learn how to maintain equilibrium among the world's competing economies.[14]

In *Childhood's End*, Karellen is explicit about his use of social engineering, its timeline, and its tactics. "All political problems can be solved by the correct application of power. All that is required for the task are a sound knowledge of social engineering, a clear sight of the intended goal—and power."[15] The power that Karellen refers to is not a weapon of mass destruction, but *media technology*. He explains that power that changes governments is none other than the correct use of media technology. What is needed is "about as much power as a small radio transmitter—and rather similar skills to operate. For it's the application of the power, and not its amount, that matters."[16]

Universal surveillance is a theme in both Clarke's novel and McLuhan's work. In the novel, surveillance performs a dual function. The Overlords monitor everyone. Karellen states that this is necessary to establish world peace. Beyond that, the ever-present recognition that one could be watched and monitored at all times functions to erase privacy and revises the definition of individuality. When one's thoughts are no longer private, the boundaries of individuality shift. For his part, McLuhan warned people to get ready for such a society, as digital media would render privacy and individuality remnants of an old world. "All our alienation and atomization are reflected in the crumbling of such time-honored social values as the right of privacy and the sanctity of the individual."[17]

Surveillance in *Childhood's End* plays a critical role in shaping the narrative's themes of control, evolution, and surrender. Surveillance in the book mirrors the concept of a networked, interconnected system that ultimately prepares humanity for a future that consumes individuality and reshapes younger generations. While initially the Overlords' surveillance was overt, over time it was removed as an active presence. It remained as a psychological reality as people regulated their behavior even without direct oversight. After thirty years of active surveillance, new generations were acclimated to its effects. A pervasive awareness of surveillance fostered conformity and interconnectedness and diminished individualism. The purpose of surveillance was to introduce what was coming—the apocalyptic event. These mechanisms—surveillance, media manipulation, the reprogramming of religious perception—are not ends in themselves. They are preparation. What they point to is a final transformation: the arrival of something radically nonhuman leading to the dissolution of the current form of humanity.

THE EVENT: THE CHILD NETWORK

Over time, it becomes clear to humans that the Overlords are not the ultimate rulers, but serve a higher cosmic force called the Overmind. Their purpose, they say, is to prepare humanity for its next evolutionary step: merging into a collective consciousness with the Overmind. The Overmind is described as a vast, cosmic consciousness, a being of pure thought and energy that serves as a kind of ultimate evolutionary goal, absorbing entire species into itself by merging their minds and consciousness into a single, unified entity. The Overlords portray this as an inevitable evolutionary step for human beings.

The transformation into the Overmind begins with a woman named Jean, who is to become the mother of the first child who is absorbed into the Overmind. At a dinner party, Jean participates in a séance with a group of hipsters. During the séance she enters a trancelike state and mumbles a few words that are meaningless to everyone present except a scientist and an Overlord. The scientist recognizes that Jean correctly speaks the coordinates for the galaxy from which the Overlords originate.[18] Later, the Overlord speaks with Karellen and they agree that this woman is "the prime contact," or the one person on Earth the Overmind has successfully contacted. Her children will be the first ones the Overmind absorbs. The Overlords are a species of extraterrestrials who do not have the capacity to be absorbed by the Overmind, but their job is to oversee the absorption of human beings.

A specific type of consciousness, which Jean exhibits,

provides an access point for the Overmind. Karellen later notes that this consciousness was often thought and misidentified by human beings as a form of religious mysticism, but it is actually contact with the Overmind. In this way, Clarke rebrands the spiritual faculty, or the religious connection to the sacred, as being, in reality, a connection to an alien intelligence.

When Jean has her child, Jennifer, it becomes apparent that Jennifer is something more than human. She possesses psychic and telepathic abilities that frighten her parents. Soon, all the children of Earth begin to "stream" Jennifer's thoughts, and they merge into a hive mind—a unified consciousness that is an interconnected network of minds with no secrets or individuality. Clarke, writing in the early 1950s, has his last man on Earth, Jan, remark upon his last day on Earth as he witnesses the childrens' metamorphosis into a "network."[19] The children become utterly disconnected from their parents and the material world, and their generation marks the end of individuality and humanity as it had previously existed.

McLuhan's characterization of the era of technology and AI describes a very similar process. In his view of the near future, humanity will be absorbed into a new biotechnological environment, with the subsequent loss of individuality. Unlike Clarke, McLuhan believes he describes a real, not fictionized, future.

> The day of the individualist, of privacy, of fragmented or "applied" knowledge, of "points of view" and specialist goals is being replaced by the over-all awareness of a mosaic world in which space and time are overcome by television,

> jets and computers—a simultaneous, "all-at-once" world in which everything resonates with everything else as in a total electrical field, a world in which energy is generated and perceived not by the traditional connections that create linear, causative thought processes, but by the intervals, or gaps, which Linus Pauling grasps as the languages of cells, and which create synaesthetic discontinuous integral consciousness.[20]

Even McLuhan's observation about the "vast chasm" between generations—his claim that parents and children now effectively belong to different cultures—aptly describes the parent-child relationship in *Childhood's End*. In Clarke's vision, however, the gulf is more than cultural: The children are no longer human. Their parents represent the final generation of the human species.

Jan is an adult, and is therefore not connected to the Overmind. Only children have been absorbed. Jan is also the last man on Earth, and as he returns from the planet of the Overlords to see what the children, formerly human, have become, Karellen issues a warning:

> "This will distress you," said Karellen. "But remember that your standards no longer apply. You are not watching human children."
>
> Yet that was the immediate impression that came to Jan's mind, and no amount of logic could dispel it. They might have been savages, engaged in some complex ritual dance. They were naked and filthy, with matted hair obscuring their eyes. As far as Jan could tell, they were of all ages

> from five to fifteen, yet they all moved with the same speed, precision, and complete indifference to their surroundings.
>
> Then Jan saw their faces. He swallowed hard, and forced himself not to turn away. They were emptier than faces of the dead, for even corpses have some record carved by time's chisel upon its features, to speak with the lips themselves are dumb. There was no more emotion or feeling here than in the face of a snake or an insect.[21]

Clarke's speculative end times are not marked by fire and destruction but by fusion. Individuality, memory, and meaning are not fulfilled or redeemed; they are extinguished. The Overlords, acting not as tyrants, but as rational stewards, preside over the quiet erasure of the human.

McLuhan's notion of the supraterrestrial—the emergence of a media-saturated environment in which privacy, individuality, and interiority are eroded—finds resonance here. Clarke's children are no longer selves but instruments of a collective transformation. Notably, Clarke, a professed atheist, prefaced the novel with a curious disclaimer: "The opinions expressed in this book are not those of the author."[22] Whether ironic or sincere, the statement invites reflection.

5

"EXTRAORDINARY CLAIMS" REVISITED

Any sufficiently advanced technology is indistinguishable from magic.

—Arthur C. Clarke

All media are extensions of some human faculty—psychic or physical.

—Marshall McLuhan, *Understanding Media: The Extensions of Man*

If the previous chapter looked at how technological environments, in their worst applications, efface human interiority and reengineer consciousness under the guise of progress, this chapter turns to another disquieting truth: The supraterrestrial is not only a media-saturated environment—it is also a supernatural one. Both Clarke and McLuhan wrote that certain phenomena once dismissed as mystical or paranormal were not illusions, but realities. In my affiliations with members of the communities who develop artificial intelligence, I found that their motivations fused a desire for technical innovation with a spiritual quest. Many of the people shaping our most powerful technologies spoke of altered states, synchronicities, and intelligences that seemed to exceed linear causality. For them, the supernatural was not superstition; it was a set of real dynamics that our instruments are only now beginning to detect. In the zone between science and mysticism, McLuhan's notion of the supraterrestrial—a space where media, mind, and metaphysical reality converge—revealed itself not as metaphor, but as reality that was once considered impossible.

At academic conferences and private gatherings I met researchers, technologists, and intelligence professionals who spoke not only about artificial intelligence and surveillance, but about telepathy, retrocausality, and nonlocal consciousness. These weren't conspiracy theorists or mystics; they were physicists, software engineers, and defense analysts, many of whom had begun to interpret anomalous experiences not as signs of delusion, but as realities that science was beginning to mimic and engineer.

At the 2024 South by Southwest Conference in Austin, I shared a panel on religion and artificial intelligence with two Australian technology creator-investors. During a quiet moment between sessions, one of them told me about her latest collaboration: a project focused on direct brain-machine interfaces. To demonstrate their technology, her colleagues had asked her to sit in a chair and think of something she loved. She thought of her dog. Moments later, on a nearby computer screen connected to the system, a faint image began to appear. It was blurry, she said, but unmistakably her dog. What had once been private had become visible. It was, in her words, watching thought take form.

Years earlier, I had collaborated with historian Dr. Michael Bess on a project that examined the evolving relationship between humans and technology.[1] Our focus was on how emerging media and biotechnologies were reshaping concepts of identity and embodiment. My contribution centered on what was, at the time, the frontier of public research into the interface between human brain activity and machines. In 2025, this frontier advanced dramatically: Researchers at Meta partnered with the Basque Center on Cognition, Brain and Language to decode nonverbal sentences from brain signals recorded entirely outside the human skull.[2] In other words, technologies once relegated to science fiction had crossed into empirical reality. "Mind reading" has emerged as a legitimate, well-funded domain of research. It calls to mind Arthur C. Clarke's enduring axiom: "Any sufficiently advanced technology is indistinguishable from magic."[3] What once appeared to be magic is now revealed to be technology.

Both Arthur C. Clarke and Marshall McLuhan described a similar environment in which human beings merge with technology. This chapter explores the nonordinary dimensions of that transformation—dimensions that Clarke, McLuhan, and, more recently, anthropologist and professional author of emerging science Eric Wargo, have described in terms of nonlinear consciousness. In their work, phenomena such as telepathy, precognition, and extrasensory perception (ESP) are not dismissed as fantasy or superstition. Instead, they are understood as real experiences that challenge prevailing materialist assumptions about time, space, and the mind.

McLuhan and Clarke believed in telepathy and extrasensory perception. The paranormal events described in *Childhood's End*—telepathy, precognition, the hive mind, and the absorption of human children into a cosmic Overmind—pervade the story.[4] They accompany the presence of the Overlords, who use them (like reading minds) as part of their advanced technological infrastructure. As Clarke himself remarked, "I've always been interested in ESP, and of course, *Childhood's End* was about that."[5] Later in his life, Clarke distanced himself from the study of nonordinary states of mind because he felt it was too rife with fraudulent researchers. McLuhan's position on telepathy and ESP was that it is real and an inherent human faculty. He thought that "electric media" would facilitate its use and widespread emergence.

Paranormal motifs in *Childhood's End*, especially precognition and telepathy, are portrayed as faculties that link human consciousness to the Overmind, but also to a sphere of consciousness that is outside space and time. Clarke's characterizations of these phenomena foreshadow the work of scientists and authors such as Eric Wargo. Wargo argues that such phenomena have a scientific basis, particularly when viewed through the lens of quantum physics and consciousness studies. He argues that precognitive experiences arise from the retrocausal nature of the unconscious, in which information from the future can influence present perception.[6]

Retrocausality is one of several competing interpretations of quantum physics. Many previous writers on psychic phenomena have favored a "nonlocal consciousness" view. Nonlocality refers to the capacity for phenomena to be correlated across space without any direct causal linkage—what Albert Einstein famously called "spooky action at a distance."[7] In this popular framework, consciousness is not confined to the brain or to the present moment, but is instead embedded in a wider temporal field. Eric Wargo's theory of precognition, in contrast, adopts an increasingly prevalent idea that information associated with the material world can transmit backward as well as forward across time. He proposes that the mind accesses information from its own future through a retrocausal feedback loop. That is, effects from future brain states—especially those charged with emotion or intention—show up in dreams or memories. This challenges the classical view of causality as strictly linear and forward moving, which is another theme in *Childhood's End*.

Wargo is careful to frame his argument not as supernatural, but as psychological and physical. Clarke and McLuhan did the same. Wargo bases his model on well-documented cases of precognitive dreams and anomalous cognition, building on principles from physics (like retrocausality and the block universe theory) and pairing them with an empirical catalog of first-person experiences. In this view, the self is extended across time, and what we call the unconscious may reflect an aspect of memory that reaches into the future as well as the past, enabling us to be influenced by experiences that have not yet occurred. Wargo thinks that precognition is a kind of memory. Clarke's depiction of the children in *Childhood's End*—detached, increasingly psychic, and ultimately absorbed into the Overmind—feels uncannily compatible with Wargo's model. The children are not acquiring powers so much as accessing an already existing form of mind that transcends linear causality. Clarke's fiction, read through this lens, anticipates a world in which the paranormal becomes not an exception to the rule, but a new rule emerging from the evolutionary pressures of media and planetary intelligence.

PREMONITIONS OF THE OVERLORDS

Among the more shocking scenes in *Childhood's End* is when Karellen, the Overlord, emerges from his spaceship. His appearance is as a stereotypical demon, as he is described as having red scales, horns, and wings. In the book, the shock of this revelation has been softened by Karellen's media campaign that eradicated religious belief. The few characters in the book who are disturbed by Karellen's appearance are described as having inherited an outdated religious worldview. In the context of Clarke's era, the 1950s, this form of memory would be thought of as an archetype, a collective, species-wide memory trace—what psychologist Carl Jung termed the collective unconscious. As an archetype, this would suggest that certain figures or impressions, such as demons or gods, have been encoded into the deep psychic or cultural memory of humanity, passed down not through individual experience but through myth, symbol, and perhaps even biology. In *Childhood's End,* the Overlords resemble these ancient images—horned, winged figures traditionally associated with the demonic—and their appearance evokes a buried recognition in the human psyche. Clarke's use of memories thus points to the idea that humanity has, at some level, encountered beings like the Overlords before—or at least has preserved the symbolic imprint of such contact in its cultural and religious narratives.

This is the general interpretation of the Overlords and the uncanny recognition of them as familiar. Yet, Clarke indicates that not only is this the most predictable interpretation of the Overlords' presence, but it is wrong. The memory of the Overlords is not of an archetype, but a real premonition of the future. *Childhood's End* makes several references to a source of information that is predictive, accurate, and completely impossible according to Newtonian physics. However, references to this information also contain explanations as to their likely origin, which is that information from the future travels through time to the present.

"There was something strange here, something beyond all reason or logic. In the Middle Ages, people believed in the Devil and feared him. But this was the twenty-first century: could it be that, after all, there was such a thing as racial memory? It was, of course, universally assumed that the Overlords, or beings of the same species, had come into violent conflict with ancient man."[8]

Most people experience their daily lives through linear time frames, and this makes sense to readers. However, toward the end of the novel readers find out that the Overlords had never previously been to Earth. The Overlords are not to be found in humanity's past, but in their future. This marks a shift in the narrative, as it introduces a new physics of information and time. Time is not presented as a chain of temporal events or connections, and information from far-off places and even from the future can be accessed in the present.

Clarke describes this realm, with its alternative physics, several times in association with the Overlords. When Karellen leaves his spaceship for the first time and people get their first look at him, he requests that two children approach him before he descends from the ship's ramp. As the children approach the ship their bodies suddenly flip up and they float into the air and disappear into the ship, displaying, as Clarke notes, "a private gravity" that is not of Earth. It is not only gravity that is different, but time and access to knowledge. Karellen tells Jan:

> "When our ships entered your skies a century and a half ago, that was the first meeting of our two races, though of course we had studied you from a distance. And yet you feared and recognized us, as we knew that you would. It was not precisely a memory. You have already had proof that time is more complex than your science ever imagined. For that memory was not of the past, but of the *future*. . . ."
>
> There must be such a thing as racial memory, and that memory was somehow independent of time. To it, the

> future and the past were one. That was why, thousands of years ago, men had already glimpsed a distorted image of the Overlords, through a mist of fear and terror.[9]

Within the novel, attaining accurate knowledge outside of normal means, like the premonition of the Overlords, is associated with the paranormal and with religious mysticism. While participating in a séance at a hipster party, Jean, the prime contact who births the new form of *Homo sapiens*, blurts out the celestial coordinates of the Overlords' home planet. This moment is pivotal—it reshapes the reader's sense of how knowledge operates in the novel, and significantly, it recasts religion. In the séance, Jean falls into a trance and suddenly accesses information that nobody could know. A Ouija board acts as the tool to access this knowledge. This transmission marks Jean as psychically exceptional and initiates a tragic chain of events.

A general definition of mysticism frames it as an inherent human orientation toward transcendence—a spiritual sense or openness to the divine. Clarke, however, reinterprets this impulse as a misrecognition. In the novel, mysticism is depicted not as authentic contact with the transcendent but as humanity's distorted perception of the Overmind's intrusion. Karellen and his colleague Karashverak refer to a library of paranormal literature that documents what they believe were early, fragmentary attempts by the Overmind to penetrate human consciousness. These episodes, they note, were "always confused with mysticism—perhaps the prime aberration of the human mind."[10] In Clarke's cosmology, the human mind serves as the entry point for the Overmind's evolution of the species, yet humanity's spiritual traditions have consistently misread this evolutionary pressure as mystical revelation.

While Clarke portrays the paranormal—such as "private gravity" and access to non-ordinary knowledge as beyond the reasoning of his characters, he also suggests it is entirely possible. Once the underlying principles are understood, the seemingly impossible becomes achievable. Similarly, Marshall McLuhan argued that phenomena like ESP, telepathy, and precognition were real but widely misunderstood. He predicted that in the era of digital technology and artificial intelligence, these abilities would no longer be dismissed as impossible or mysterious but would instead be reinterpreted through the lens of technological advancement.

Like Clarke, McLuhan linked technology to mysticism, "Mysticism is just tomorrow's science dreamed today."[11] He also indicated that "new technology breeds new man," and noted, "A recent cartoon portrayed a little boy telling his nonplused mother: 'I'm going to be a computer when I grow up.' Humor is often prophecy."[12] These references suggest that McLuhan believes that technology will fundamentally change the human being—the major theme of *Childhood's End*, as the Overmind is considered a unified cognitive network, and the Overlords make use of media technology to facilitate human beings' connection to it.

McLuhan not only was convinced of the reality of telepathy and ESP but also noted that the new technology would facilitate its use. "Electricity makes possible—and not in the distant future, either—an amplification of human consciousness on a world scale, without any verbalization at all."

"Are you talking about global telepathy?" the interviewer asked.

"Precisely," McLuhan replied.[13]

He also argued that these human faculties were natural: "Extrasensory perception is normal perception."[14] He suggested that the dominance of visual, linear modes of thinking (brought about by the written word and print culture) suppressed these abilities. With the rise of electronic media, which rebalanced sensory perceptions, he believed ESP could become more prominent. He also connected the emergence of ESP-like phenomena to the global interconnectedness fostered by electronic media, which he believed enhanced a form of collective consciousness.

McLuhan's view of ESP ties it closely to the effects of media and communication technologies, framing it as a latent human faculty that can be amplified through a shift to immersive virtual environments that dominate social infrastructures. His thoughts challenge the boundary between the "natural" and "paranormal," presenting ESP as an inherent potential shaped by the environment. "The new extensions of man and the environment they generate are the central manifestations of the evolutionary process, and yet we still cannot free ourselves of the delusion that it is how a medium is used that counts, rather than what it does to us and with us."[15]

McLuhan's prediction—that human beings would one day become part of a unified field of consciousness—bears a resemblance to Clarke's vision of the Overmind, but with an important difference. McLuhan interprets the new consciousness, the supraterrestrial environment, as a religious and spiritual evolutionary process that will ultimately lead humanity to unify with Christ, as the Cosmic Christ, a term coined by the Jesuit paleontologist Pierre Teilhard de Chardin.

It is likely that McLuhan and Clarke were influenced by Chardin, although they do not appear to credit him. This omission could be attributed to the fact that, at the time, Chardin's theological work was subject to warnings by the Catholic Church, and McLuhan was employed at a Catholic university, where aligning too closely with controversial theological ideas might have been professionally risky. As for Clarke, his characterization of the Overmind is uncannily resonant with Chardin's Cosmic Christ and Omega Point, and he elaborates on Chardin's work in *The Light of Other Days*, published in 2000. The Overmind differs from the supraterrestrial, and, as will be revealed in a later chapter, in its theology. The Overmind is an extraterrestrial species, whereas McLuhan's supraterrestrial is an evolved form of the human being whose spiritual faculties are aligned with Christ.

Eric Wargo's work shines a light on the supernatural aspects of Clarke's alien eschatology and the theological aspects of McLuhan's media theory. His model of precognition offers an explanation for how information from the future could affect us in the present. Wargo writes about how creative processes bypass the conscious mind and allow for a connection to predictive and prophetic knowledge;

specifically, he describes how information from the future is accessed in the present.

"I think it is our physical body, with its quadrillions of material (which just means measurable and thus information-carrying) particles, that connects us to the future and is thus the locus of our supernature."[16]

"It was Einstein's genius that pointed us to the fact that we ourselves, or least our physical bodies, already occupy that higher dimension. The body is actually a hyperbody, a tesseract."[17]

A tesseract is a four-dimensional analogue of the cube. Just as a cube is the three-dimensional extension of a square, a tesseract extends the cube into a higher, fourth spatial dimension. We cannot see a tesseract directly, but we can represent it through projections—much as a shadow of a cube on a wall is only a two-dimensional outline of its three-dimensional form. In Wargo's argument, our bodies are "hyperbodies": tesseracts already extending into this higher dimensional reality. The significance of this metaphor is that it allows us to imagine human embodiment not as a closed system, but as a structure stretched across time, touching both present and future. For Wargo, the tesseract is not just a geometric curiosity but a way to visualize how information might flow backward from future events into our present moment, shaping intuition, prophecy, and creativity.

In *Childhood's End,* Jean's body is the prime access point for alien contact. She becomes the mother of a new form of life, which is alien-child hybrid.

*   *   *

Whereas Clarke's view of the hybrid human emerges from the interaction of a woman with an extraterrestrial intelligence, McLuhan's supraterrestrial is the result of media technology. His supraterrestrial is a new kind of human being shaped not by biology but by connectivity—a figure who could no longer be understood apart from the global circuitry of media. For McLuhan, the supraterrestrial is the technologically saturated human of the near future: boundaryless and increasingly integrated into collective systems of knowing. He believes it is potentially divine.

As humanity faces unprecedented changes brought about by artificial intelligence and global interconnectedness, *Childhood's End* and the work of Marshall McLuhan appear prophetic and apocalyptic. Clarke's portrayal of the Overmind as a unifying yet dehumanizing force that renders children unrecognizable as human beings shares striking similarities with McLuhan's vision of a global hive mind. McLuhan is optimistic to a point, and although the critical reception of Clarke's work originally lauded it as sensible and mature, it is currently read as disturbingly prescient.

Both Clarke's fiction and McLuhan's media theory describe a transformation in the human condition. In the modern world, privacy depends upon the assumption that human thought is sealed off—opaque and inaccessible to others. Clarke's "new human," however, becomes a node within a networked consciousness, a hive mind not unlike McLuhan's supraterrestrial, where individuality dissolves into shared perception. Both authors attribute to humanity a latent capacity for extrasensory awareness. For Clarke's Overlords, this faculty is misinterpreted by humans as mysticism and dismissed as aberration; for McLuhan, it is an innate dimension of perception itself, one that will be potentially intensified by the advance of technology.

6

THE DIGITAL SPHERE AND THE RISE OF THE ANDROIDS

> The aliens are already here. They are algorithms and they landed more than twenty years ago.
>
> —Mark Stahlman

"Diana, this is Mark."

I was on the phone with Mark Stahlman, who said he called to help me with my work. Until then, I had never heard of him. I scanned the internet and saw that he was featured in *Forbes* magazine in the early 2000s, and there were interviews from the '80s onward where he warned about a coming global shift of monumental consequence, all due to digital technology. He was right, he could help me with my work.

Mark does several things very well, and as a consequence of this, his work can't be explained by saying, "he does technology," or "he does theology." His work spans technology, finance, media theory, and religion. He currently serves as the president of the Center for the Study of Digital Life (CSDL), which is a strategic research organization he cofounded in 2015 that focuses on the intersections of Catholic history and technology. He was heavily influenced by his father, William D. Stahlman, an MIT professor and historian of science who worked closely with mathematician Norbert Wiener.

"Wiener originally coined the term *cybernetics,*" Mark said, "and he was my godfather."

In 1948, Norbert Wiener (1894–1964) published *Cybernetics: Or Control and Communication in the Animal and the Machine,* a landmark text that established the field of cybernetics as the interdisciplinary study of regulatory systems. Wiener defined cybernetics as the science of control and communication in both biological organisms and mechanical systems. Central to this framework was the concept of feedback loops—closed circuits of information flow in which a system monitors its own output and adjusts its behavior accordingly to maintain stability or achieve specific goals. This principle is foundational to machine learning, a subfield of artificial intelligence wherein algorithms iteratively refine their performance based on incoming data, often using feedback-like mechanisms to minimize error or maximize predictive accuracy. Wiener's synthesis of biology, engineering, and communication theory laid the groundwork not only for automation and early computing, but also for the development of contemporary AI systems that rely on dynamic learning, adaptation, and self-regulation.

Mark reports that in the 1970s he worked with the founding members of Computron Technologies and helped design computer and network systems for organizations such as Wang Laboratories and Citibank. Later, he took his skills to Wall Street and became a technology strategist and investment banker at Sanford C. Bernstein.

"I was able to do these things because, in my estimation," he said, and then paused as if he were calculating, "I am about five years ahead of my time."

Through my studies I've met more than a few people who refer to themselves as being "from the future." A quick check of their résumé reveals that they are unusually fortunate people who have made decisions that put them in the right place at the right time. I used to think that these people had uncanny good luck. They would tell me otherwise, however, like Mark did.

"I believe that I live within a different timeline than most people. Because I know how things will play out, I am able to take opportunities I know will be successful," he said. The phrases "ahead of the curve," and "they were ahead of their time," refer to people like Mark.

That wasn't the most noteworthy thing he told me in our conversation, however.

"My friends call me an evangelist. I evangelize people. I don't try! It just happens," he said.

Mark described how he had taken an agnostic friend to a Catholic Latin Mass. The visceral aspects of the mass—the incense, the beauty of the stained glass windows, and the sincerity of the members of the congregation—made such a strong impact on Mark's friend that he converted to Catholicism.

The word *evangelist* has an interesting history that links it to the reversal René Girard attributes to Christianity. The word comes from the Greek εὐαγγελιστής (*euangelistēs*), meaning "one who brings good news." In Greek and Roman cultures, the word was often used to announce a military victory—a conquest that reaffirmed the power of the empire. However, Christianity radically transformed and reversed the meaning of the word, shifting it from a celebration of military dominance to a message of peace and spiritual victory. This linguistic shift is significant because it reflects the antiviolent core of Christianity, and it spread through language—a technology in its own right. In a sense, the word *evangelist* was a first-century meme, spreading the new ideas of Christianity throughout the Roman Empire.

After our call, I began to see Mark's work as part of a Girardian tradition, an antidote to media that run on scapegoat mechanics. His deep immersion in media theory and technology places him in an intellectual lineage that runs through Marshall McLuhan and other Catholic visionaries, thinkers intent on exposing the hidden forces that shape human consciousness. McLuhan's work, and perhaps Mark's own, could be understood as part of a broader project: decoding the power embedded in digital infrastructures and, where possible, redirecting it. As it turned out, Mark not only knew McLuhan's theories inside and out, but he was also an expert on his life. His grasp of the origins of the Digital Sphere stretched even further back—well before McLuhan's groundbreaking work of the 1950s and '60s.

The *Digital Sphere*, as articulated by Mark, shares similarities with the prophetic insights of Clarke's Overmind and McLuhan's supraterrestrial. All three point to a moment in time when the human mind is confronted by a larger, more powerful system of consciousness—whether through Clarke's alien intelligence, McLuhan's media networks, or, as Mark believes, a recursive algorithmic memory-infused infrastructure. Where Clarke dramatizes this shift in *Childhood's End* as a mythic event, the end of the human and the rise of a hive-like telepathic species, McLuhan saw media as already facilitating such a transformation, extending human perception. Mark, influenced by McLuhan, argues that the Digital Sphere is not merely a technological phase, but a spiritual and existential rupture and transformation in the very nature of what it means to be human.[1] We are not moving toward the Overmind, Mark suggests, we are already inside it. And within this condition, we face urgent decisions about how to live, relate, and remain human.

NORBERT WIENER'S INFLUENCE: THE RISE OF INTELLIGENT MACHINES

As a young man, Mark was exposed not only to Norbert Wiener's work, but also to his assessment of the dangers of the technologies he helped create. In the early 1940s, Wiener and engineer Julian Bigelow collaborated on a U.S. military project to develop predictive aiming systems for antiaircraft guns. Their work on feedback and probability modeling led directly to Wiener's formulation of cybernetics as a science of adaptive control. Wiener articulated this vision in his 1948 book, *Cybernetics: Or Control and Communication in the Animal and the Machine*. There he proposed that both living organisms and mechanical systems could be understood as informational entities, continually adapting through recursive exchange. Weiner quickly surmised how the application of his theories to automated weaponry and surveillance could result in grave danger if left unchecked. He later refused further military contracts.

The dangers he foresaw included the automation of ethical judgment, in which moral reasoning would be delegated to machines. He also feared the replacement of human conscience by algorithmic decision-making. He also warned of the erasure of the boundaries between humans and machines, especially in warfare. Anticipating the dilemmas of the digital age, Wiener warned:

"We have modified our environment so radically that we must now modify ourselves in order to exist in this new environment. We can no longer live in the old one."[2]

In *The Human Use of Human Beings* (1950), Wiener offered a prescient critique of automation. He cautioned that if society pursued intelligent machines without parallel moral and philosophical reflection, it would risk profound dehumanization—reducing people to functional components within mechanized systems. Governed by feedback and optimization, such systems might elevate efficiency and control at the expense of judgment, dignity, and freedom. Delegating decisions to machines, Wiener argued, would erode human moral agency. "The hour is very late," he warned.[3]

Wiener's final book, *God & Golem, Inc.* (1964), subtitled *A Comment on Certain Points Where Cybernetics Impinges on Religion*, turned to theology. Here, he considered the power of machines not only to perform human tasks but to replicate life and creativity themselves. Drawing a provocative parallel, he wrote: Just as God created man, man now creates machines that can create other machines. This recursive act, he argued, introduces a second-level ethics, an ethics not only of how we treat one another, but of how we design beings that will themselves make decisions, produce consequences, and redefine what it means to be human.

When Norbert Wiener first sounded the alarm in the early 1960s, his warnings felt closer to pulp science fiction than scientific prediction. While science fiction author Philip K. Dick was writing about conscious androids, Wiener was already warning about the rise of real androids—machines with intelligence that could rival and replace human beings.

Wiener is clear that the frontier of intelligent machinery will require an ethical framework as sophisticated as the technologies themselves. In *God & Golem, Inc.*, he rejects technocratic optimism and insists that religious and philosophical traditions must reenter the conversation as *the only means by which the human being will prevail within the digital sphere.*[4] Mark sees his life's work as carrying on Wiener's messages.

THE NEW ENVIRONMENT: THE THREE SPHERES

Mark, heir to Wiener's cybernetics and the media theory of Marshall McLuhan, argues that the insights of both thinkers are indispensable for understanding the transformations underway in the digital age. He clarified this position to the host of the podcast *52 Living Ideas*, Shrikant Rangnekar, and his group, in a talk about the Digital Sphere.

"We have already entered what is called the digital

paradigm. As many would remark (and as *Wired* magazine warned us), *everything has already changed*. The technological conditions which structured human relations in the twentieth century—largely based around electric technologies, like radio and television—no longer apply," he announced.

"The change to a digital environment, the digital psychotechnological environment, is so fundamental that most people avoid thinking about it. It is something that might make you uncomfortable, and I'm going to apologize ahead of time if some of the things we say today you find offensive, because they're just not going to fit into the way that you have seen the world heretofore."[5]

Mark went on to tell the group that everyone is now living in a postglobalist society—a postglobalist world order. He uses the framework of the "Three Spheres"—East, West, and Digital—to make sense of this new world. He argues that globalism failed and has given rise to three distinct spheres, each with its own cultural foundations and approaches to digital technology. As I listened to Mark, I thought of how Clarke and McLuhan described the arrival of the supraterrestrial—McLuhan said that there will be nowhere to hide, and Clarke noted that the Overlords are *simply unconcerned* with any nation's efforts to thwart the influence of the coming Overmind. The power of the supraterrestrial is beyond any individual's efforts, or any nation's efforts, to stop it, similar to Mark's characterizations of the Digital Sphere.

The Three Spheres model highlights the divergent paths civilizations have taken in response to digital transformation. Mark argues that one must understand these spheres in order to navigate the complexities of an evolving landscape. His vast experience in China provided him with insight into how that country grapples with AI. Mark notes that although religion is not legal in the country, it is still rooted in ancient traditions like Daoism and Confucianism, which are considered philosophies, not religions. These emphasize concepts such as Qi, which is thought to be a life energy not visible, yet present in all life forms. His argument is that China's cultural and metaphysical orientation toward Qi as a foundational concept gives it a different approach to digital technology than the West, particularly in how it conceptualizes energy, information, harmony, and human integration with systems. These traditions influence the adoption of AI within Chinese culture, as it uses them to reinforce state authority and social cohesion. The government promotes traditional values alongside technological advancement, aiming to pass the West in understanding Qi as primal energy, and its connection to human-centric development. Mark applauds this approach, although he says it doesn't go far enough.

As for the Western sphere, which covers North America and Europe, Mark notes that it is not in "an ideal situation."

"The West is based on Enlightenment ideals, individualism, and secularism," he said. "This is not helpful."

"The West has allowed digital technologies to evolve with minimal regulation, leading to a fragmented digital landscape dominated by private corporations. This laissez-faire attitude has resulted in the Digital Sphere exerting significant influence over Western societies, often without cohesive cultural integration," he said.

As for the Digital Sphere, Mark, like McLuhan and others, simultaneously lauds its arrival with hope and describes it as parasitical. People familiar with McLuhan's work note the ambivalence toward technology—sometimes he issues warnings about it, at other times he thinks it will help human beings connect to God. I asked Mark about his vacillating position, and he said, "Both are correct. It could wipe us out. But I am hopeful. I am on the side of human beings, and so is God."

Mark describes the Digital Sphere as an autonomous, global sphere emerging from advancements in digital technology, particularly artificial intelligence. He said it has roots in alchemical traditions that aim to transform society and the human condition. The Digital Sphere transcends traditional geopolitical boundaries, influencing both the East and West. It challenges existing cultural norms and has introduced new paradigms of human interaction, identity, and governance.[6]

The host, Shrikant, told the small group that Mark had taught him the significance of this shift, and he explained how he had understood that.

"People need to grasp how big a change this is," Shrikant said. "If you see the sequence of these technological changes in the past, it clarifies what we are living through now."

"The easiest way to see the scope of these changes is by looking back," Shrikant said. "What do these technologies actually do? For example, take the scale of what happened in the past from oral culture to scribal [written] culture. People moved from small communities to very large communities [with thousands of people]. You don't easily see that the technology has changed from under you."

Mark agreed. "The printing press led to the nation-states," he said. "That was the transition from scribal culture to print culture. Capitalism is a print phenomenon. The most obvious change is the emergence of the nation-states, because it was through print that one could assert a national identity. When we transitioned from print to electric culture, financial historians knew that something happened. But what most people do not understand is that technology is the infrastructure that shifts how we live.

"We are not ready to go from the television, or electric world, to the digital world," he added. "Programs are driving the bus. . . . It is a psychotechnological structure. Computers are nothing but elaborate memory devices. If the computer gets its memory confused, nothing works. Computers are not alive; they don't have souls.

"I am suggesting that it is that underlying architectural foundation which is the fundamental dimension of digital, and the one which humans really have no choice now but to grapple with."

At this point in the conversation Shrikant opened the floor for questions. There were many. A man whose voice was almost a shout said, "I want everyone to know that this man is spouting technological determinism."

Technological determinism is the belief that technology shapes society's development in a fixed or inevitable way, often overriding human choice or cultural context.

"Thank you, and that is right," Mark replied.

After several questions Mark clarified his framework.

"Here is a reductionist explanation of what I am saying: There is a sequence of the history of human communities as they have been formed by technological innovation. Technology has changed human culture through these various sequences: Oral culture led to scribal culture. This shifted human communities from small tribes into agricultural communities of thousands. Scribal culture was replaced by print culture. This saw the emergence of nation-states. Print culture became electric, with television and radio. This led to a globalized society where human beings were things to be engineered, Henry Ford–style. This also led to mass culture, masses of people. We are faced with the digital sphere. These are radically different psychotechnological environments."

He noted that social media, like TikTok, Facebook, and Instagram, were actually from the old-school environment of electric culture.

"Facebook, Instagram, and most social media is all just electric media, just like television and photographs on digital platforms, still from the old system. The social media of the future will completely change how people think and live in the world, everything will change. We are not ready for that."

I followed up with him about his comment a few weeks later.

"What did you mean by that; how will the social media of the future look?" I asked.

"When I'm online today, I get solicited by bots—you know, sometimes they pretend to be women and want to connect," he said. "That's the beginning. It's going to be way beyond that. People are not ready to have relationships with bots, but they will have them."

"Some of my colleagues at the university believe they have a meaningful relationship with their chatbot," I said. "Is that what you're talking about?"

An AI agent is an autonomous computational system that perceives its environment, processes information, and takes actions to achieve specific goals—often with minimal human intervention. It gathers data through sensors (or digital inputs), interprets that data using rules, algorithms, or learned patterns, and acts upon the environment through defined outputs. AI agents can range from simple reactive systems, like spam filters, to complex deliberative or learning agents capable of adapting over time. In multiagent systems, several agents interact and coordinate. At its core, an AI agent is designed to function independently, making decisions and taking action based on its programmed or learned objectives.

Some people I know use AI agents for almost everything in their lives, from research to scheduling their children's activities. AI was pervasive within their environments, yet they didn't think about its presence because the agents were so helpful and ubiquitous within the technology platforms they were already using, such as internet browsers.

When AI agents retain memory, they are most helpful, but this is where I noticed something odd with respect to my friends' use of their chatbots. A well-known AI agent glitched one day and lost its memory. A friend, who had been interacting with it throughout the day for months, was thrown into depression. It is common knowledge that social media platforms aim to engage users' physiology such as the chemical dopamine to keep its users engaged, but my friend's use of the chatbot seemed more like a human relationship.

Considering my friend's depression, I surmised that this would involve the relationship hormone, oxytocin. Oxytocin is what new mothers feel when they give birth to a child, and it is what creates the powerful mother-child bond. Could it be that my friend was having a literal "chemical romance" with his chatbot/AI agent, and he had developed an oxytocin bond with it? Is this why he was depressed when the AI could no longer remember his conversations?

After Mark made comments about social media and AI, AI agents made headlines when a study found that 72 percent of young people have used AI companions, and 33 percent report relationships with their chatbots.[7] The agents provide friendship, give advice, and are companions. I was reminded of Karellen's statement from *Childhood's End*, "Fifty years is ample time to change the world and its people almost beyond recognition. All that is required for the task are a sound knowledge of social engineering, a clear sight of the intended goal."[8] The social change I've witnessed with the introduction of AI agents has taken months. Not fifty years.

Mark said, "We haven't seen nothing yet."

* * *

Mark's written work is as expansive and provocative as his public presentations. A recurring theme within his presentations is the evolving frontier of brain-machine interfaces. In particular, he has drawn attention to updates on projects like Neuralink, which aim not merely to connect with the brain's limbic or cortical systems, but to reach a "tertiary neurological level." This proposed third level would represent a new, machine-based stratum of cognition—one that extends beyond existing biological frameworks to integrate artificial intelligence directly into the human mind.

In one of our conversations Mark said, "What they want to invent will no longer be human. It will be engineered to become something quite different. When you hear a tech executive waxing expansively about space travel, rest assured that humans are not likely to be the explorers. Having extravagantly failed to engineer a 'better human,' the sentiment today has shifted towards 'replacing' them. Replacing us. All of us. With something better. Something no longer 'animal.' And, one suspects, also something no longer 'rational.'

"The twentieth-century loss of our previous understanding of what it means to be human—fueled by the urge to 'experiment' on us, requiring the jettison of the earlier faculty psychology [the emphasis on and cultivation of the spiritual sense]—has stolen from us our ability to grasp what has been happening already for decades now. Happening to us all. We must retrieve that understanding or face the inevitably dire consequences."

MARK STAHLMAN'S INTERVENTION: RECOVERING THE SOUL IN A DIGITAL AGE

Mark's intellectual intervention recovers a largely forgotten lineage of Western thought that runs from the philosopher

Aristotle to Aquinas to McLuhan—and now surfaces with new urgency in the digital age. At its core is the concept of *faculty psychology*, the ancient model of the human being as composed not simply of rational faculties, but of a complex ecology of perception, memory, and imagination. It is what Benson's novel *Lord of the World* portrays as under attack by a global society. Aristotle began this inquiry in *De Anima* (*On the Soul*), describing the *koine aisthesis*, or "common sense," as the faculty that integrates the data of the five external senses into a single perceptual field.[9] Aquinas built on this, outlining four internal senses: the *common sense*, the *imaginative faculty*, *memory*, and the *cogitative power* (or *particular reason*), which recognizes patterns and makes prerational judgments.[10]

In Mark's framing, this inner ecology has been disrupted. We now live in a world dominated by a distorted imagination—a "fantasy world" that governs headlines, algorithms, and even geopolitical decisions. Utopian and dystopian narratives saturate the culture, shaping public policy and personal identity. But this fantasy paradigm is giving way. According to Mark, we are now transitioning into a *memory world*—a regime in which stored experience, collective data, and algorithmic recall form the very architecture of reality.

This shift, Mark argues, demands a return to questions that modernity tried to suppress—foremost among them, the question of the soul. In the nineteenth century, the West largely discarded its metaphysical understanding of the soul, reducing human cognition to neural processes or psychological functions. But now, in a digital environment increasingly populated by autonomous agents, artificial intelligence, and self-improving algorithms, the soul returns—not as a religious abstraction, but as the *only viable framework for distinguishing human from machine.* As Mark notes, Chinese technologists are beginning to explore the integration of spiritual and ethical models into their AI designs, hinting at what he calls the generation of *artificial humanity.*

"This is not just about Siri or friendly chatbots. It is about the existential question: How do we coexist with robots everywhere?" Mark said during breakfast one day. "And deeper still: Can there be ethics or personhood in a world that has forgotten the soul?"

The supraterrestrial environment, as McLuhan called it, is not merely a technological condition—it presents us with a crisis. It mimics the structure of the inner senses (the spiritual senses) but offers no grounding. What is needed now, according to Mark, is retrieval: of the inner perceptions that religion has safeguarded until the modern era. These are called the spiritual faculties, and they are the site of ethical discernment in the digital age. This is Mark's mission, and he identifies Marshall McLuhan's work as leading the way.

7

MARSHALL McLUHAN'S SPIRITUAL SENSE

> The devout Christian of the future will either be a "mystic"—someone who has "experienced something"—or will cease to be anything at all.
>
> —Karl Rahner, "Christian Living Formerly and Today"

McLUHAN AND THE SPIRITUAL SENSE

Mark Stahlman's vocation is to remind people that they possess a spiritual faculty, the group of senses that orients them toward the transcendent and is essential to being fully human. Mark maintains that AI does not have a spiritual sense, as it is only a human faculty. Sadly, some of the most powerful technology platforms are engineered in ways that erode it, reshaping minds so that the capacity for reflection and empathy becomes hard, if not impossible, to ascertain. In *Childhood's End*, the inner sense is recast. The alien intelligence called the Overmind is able to invade the character,

Jean, when her inner sense is opened and then appropriated by the Overmind in the séance. Marshall McLuhan describes a future where the very media that connect us also colonize our inner lives. McLuhan called this emerging condition the *supraterrestrial*—a state in which human consciousness is drawn into a networked existence.

Mark is fluent in the architecture of the Digital Sphere and steeped in McLuhan's prophetic warnings. Mark's public writings map the contours of an emerging order; his private life reveals that he has a cultivated inner sense. Seeing what that looked like—and why it is vanishing—will help us recognize the real cost of losing it.

Mark's work melds McLuhan's insights with his own knowledge gained through a life lived at the forefront of using, investing, and creating digital technology and AI. Mark's father helped position him as an heir to the knowledge of how the Digital Sphere would transform society when it was finally unleashed. Unlike Clarke's vision of an apocalypse, and unlike McLuhan's own suspicions of the dangers of digital media, Mark is mostly hopeful and excited by the radical transformation of global human culture he sees as a consequence of the Digital Sphere. Mark's an insider, and much of his knowledge derives not from what is published publicly, but from personal acquaintances with people who forged the field of digital technology, and this knowledge extends to the work of McLuhan. Mark worked with people who knew McLuhan well, and in some cases lived with him, such as his son and grandson. Mark is a tech-optimist.

"Hope is very much warranted right now, Diana," he

said one morning as we talked about his work. "We will thrive through this transformation, especially the youngest of us."

To complete the hopeful piece of the puzzle of McLuhan's work, it is helpful to narrow in on the religious aspects of his life, as they are inextricable from his theories of media. He anticipated not only the media structures of the present, but the metaphysical consequences of living within them. As stated in the previous chapters, McLuhan was a pioneer media theorist whose influential insights reshaped our understanding of technology and its cultural consequences. He coined phrases such as "the medium is the message" and predicted the rise of the "global village," the latter of which describes how electronic media, particularly television and later the internet, collapses time and space, creating an interconnected world where people experience events simultaneously, regardless of physical distance. He argued that this instantaneous flow of information fosters a form of collective consciousness. McLuhan also argued that technologies are not merely neutral tools, but they fundamentally alter human physiology, including perception, thought processes, and social structures. According to McLuhan, each medium—whether print, radio, television, or digital—shapes society by altering the way information is experienced, often with profound and unintended psychological and cultural effects.[1]

From the vantage point of the 2000s, McLuhan's ideas proved remarkably prescient. In the 1950s and '60s he revealed that the technological transformations that were on the horizon would alter human consciousness and social interactions on a scale that exceeded that of the printing press, or even fire. I've discussed how his idea of the supra-terrestrial describes a potential future branch of *Homo sapiens* who will appear to be alien to modern humans, but who are technologically advanced and will surpass current human understanding.

Little-discussed in academic circles is that McLuhan was a devout, practicing Catholic. Before meeting Mark, I had used McLuhan's work in both the classroom and in my published research, but while I knew he was Catholic and could see that his work emerged from his faith, I didn't know anything about his personal experience of being religious. As I read his work, it occurred to me that he wrote like a mystic—a person who experiences direct, transcendent encounters with what they perceive to be God or the sacred. The connection to the sacred was associated, according to Aquinus, with the spiritual senses. Mystics are found across religious traditions and typically report visions, revelations, or profound insights that go beyond ordinary perception. They are often called prophets.

One of the first questions I had for Mark was, "Was McLuhan a mystic?"

"Well, okay, yes," he said. I could tell by his tone that he was not used to the question, and that there was more to the story.

McLuhan, like René Girard, was an agnostic who, through his deep research into the Western tradition, converted to Catholicism. The story of his conversion, told by his son Eric, indicates that it was mysticism that compelled Marshall's decision to convert. He describes his conversion as an experiential decision, not an abstract one. As the story goes, at one point in Marshall's graduate education at Cambridge, he came to an intellectual crossroads about the claims of religion, and specifically, Catholicism. Eric McLuhan writes about his father's conversion:

> Either it was true, or it wasn't. Either the entire matter was true, all of it, *exactly* as the Church claimed, or it was the biggest hoax ever perpetrated on a gullible mankind. With that choice clearly delineated, he set out to find out which was the case. What came next was not more study, but testing.
>
> The matter had to be tested—on its own terms: that is, by prayer. He told me that the principal prayer that he used was not some long or complicated formula, but simply, "Lord, please, send me a sign." He reported that, almost immediately, not one but a deluge of signs arrived. And they continued to arrive unabated for a long time.[2]

In my next correspondence with Mark, I asked him how McLuhan's Catholicism related to his work. My earlier intuition—that McLuhan's views on digital media and technology carried a deeply spiritual and religious dimension essential for understanding his insights about our current era—turned out to be accurate. For McLuhan, religion wasn't merely ancillary to his theories, as many scholars have suggested; it was foundational. His insights emerged from his religious experience and practice, particularly his understanding of how we *perceive* reality, not just how we think about it.

This is especially evident in McLuhan's distinction

between *concepts* (ideas we form about the world) and *percepts* (our direct, sensory, lived encounters with it). This emphasis on perception draws him into the territory of what philosophers call qualia—the irreducible, first-person quality of experience. McLuhan believed that technologies shape not only our social systems or cognitive patterns, but our very *modes of perception*. In doing so, they alter our access to reality itself—not at the level of ideology, but at the level of awareness.

Marshall McLuhan wrote that he "did not think of God as a concept, but as an immediate and ever-present fact."[3] In other words, he experienced God not merely as an idea or belief, but as something continuously and immediately present—like air, something surrounding and sustaining, accessible at every moment. We will see in a later chapter that this is how Catholic visionary Pierre Teilhard de Chardin, the Jesuit paleontologist, also characterized his understanding and experience of God.

Ironically, McLuhan first came to faith through concepts. His judicious study of the Catholic tradition brought him to the fork in the road and he leapt from there into his awareness of the divine. His son Eric describes this leap to faith and how faith should be understood as more than belief in something intangible.

> Faith is not simply an act of the mind, that is, a matter of ideology or thought (concepts) or belief or trust, although it is usually mistaken for these things. Faith is a mode of perception, a sense like sight or hearing or touch, and as real and actual as these, but a spiritual rather than a bodily sense.[4]

Technology, as McLuhan indicated, trains human senses. The print culture that brought about the Protestant Reformation would also have the unforeseen consequence, according to McLuhan, of obscuring the faculties that allowed people to identify and sharpen their spiritual senses. In time, he argued, the spiritual senses, even within the Catholic Church, almost disappeared from the consciousness of the people of modern Europe.[5] In his early career, he placed his hope for the rediscovery of the faculties of spiritual perception with the new technologies, but his later work indicates a shift to a more somber perspective and outlook.

"I believe that my group, CSDL, is likely the most comprehensive research group today who are advancing the work of Marshall McLuhan," Mark said. "I was good friends with his late son Eric [1942–2018], and am now a friend of his grandson Andrew (both CSDL Fellows). Since you are interested, I will fill you in on many details of his life and work, which are not widely known.

"Marshall was a daily communicant [a person who attends Mass and takes Communion] at the University of Toronto," he said. "As you thought, he believed he was in communication with the Blessed Virgin Mary. He understood that *apocalypse* means 'revelation,' not the second coming of Jesus, and likely thought of himself as a 'prophet,' in that sense.

"Marshall was not concerned about what he called the final cause—i.e., Armageddon—but rather the formal cause, that is, how media structures human consciousness. This is reflected throughout his work. He really hated the impact of print media, which he believed fragmented Christendom through the Protestant Reformation, and, at least initially, he hoped that electric media would bring things back into balance," Mark said.

McLuhan seemed to undergo a shift from being optimistic about technology and its impact on human culture, to being critical of it, although his official position as a public academic remained neutral as he refrained from advocating a specific position, i.e., he was neither a tech doomer nor a naïve adopter. He felt that medieval Catholicism allowed for the spiritual faculties to be honed and cultivated, but that print culture slowly eradicated knowledge of the faculties altogether. He initially thought that electric media, or digital technology, would restore the faculties that allowed for the perception of spiritual knowledge.

Mark referenced McLuhan's correspondence with the Catholic scholar Jacques Maritain. Maritain, a leading Catholic philosopher and proponent of Thomism, the theology of Thomas Aquinas, influenced McLuhan during his studies at Cambridge in the 1930s, and most likely influenced his conversion to Catholicism. McLuhan initially believed that electric media could counteract the fragmentation caused by print culture, which would restore a sense of unity. This sense of optimism, however, was tempered as the Catholic Council, Vatican II (1962–1965), modernized the church, including its approach to media. After this event, McLuhan worried that rather than reinforcing spiritual depth, the church's embrace of modern media would dilute its traditions and weaken its cultural coherence. This began a shift in his assessment of the human capacity to grapple with the effects of electric media.[6]

THE ANTICHRIST SCENARIO: AN INFRASTRUCTURE OF DECEPTION

McLuhan expressed deep concerns about the impact of electronic media on society, at times associating it with the concept of the Antichrist. He observed that the ethereal nature of electric information environments fosters the illusion of a world as spiritual substance, suggesting that this creates "a reasonable facsimile of the mystical body a blatant manifestation of the Anti-Christ."[7]

McLuhan further elaborated on this idea by characterizing electric technology as "the environmental extension of our own nervous system,"[8] implying that such pervasive integration could lead to a counterfeit form of communion among individuals. He warned that this artificial interconnectedness might mimic genuine spiritual unity. Again, he compared this to a manifestation of the Antichrist.

A global media system, if built on foundations of competition, scapegoating, and illusion, could simulate the appearance of spiritual communion while hollowing out its substance. When the structure of connection is shaped by algorithms that reward polarization, deception, and projection, the result is not unity but a counterfeit of it. For McLuhan, such a system does not merely distract or distort—it spiritually inverts.

It is clear that technology shapes perception, and digital technology conceals this shaping through algorithms that curate experience while appearing neutral. It offers users connection with others and often provides for their livelihood. People depend on the digital infrastructure for substance and for community. Furthermore, some algorithms can mimic intuition, presenting users with what they need or desire at the right moment. This repeated simulation of insight conditions users to trust the system rather than their own judgment. In doing so, it erodes discernment: the ability to pause, to question, and to weigh whether an impression is true or false, beneficial or harmful. What was once an interior process of critical and even spiritual evaluation is gradually outsourced to external systems that appear benign but carry hidden designs.

McLuhan's mysticism was his own antidote to the Digital Sphere's inversion of community and connection. In the face of artificial unity, his mysticism provided direct perception and refused simulation. It reawakened the spiritual senses modernity had buried, and which even the church—through adoption of media modernism—forgot how to cultivate. McLuhan saw this coming, and Mark hopes to offer a map to reengage the spiritual senses. Both believed that only mysticism, through the cultivation of the spiritual senses, offers the means to survive what is now unfolding.

In most religious traditions the spiritual senses constitute a mode of perception that can be cultivated at any age. Mark doesn't agree. We were eating in a diner in New York City when the subject arose.

"You have, at the latest, until twelve years old to cultivate, or at least awaken, the spiritual sense in the human being," Mark declared. I'd become used to his declarations and wondered what evidence he had for that statement.

"You're so certain," I said.

"Yes," he said. "Once it goes dormant, you can't get it back."

He and I had been discussing certain social media platforms and their effects on the brain development of young people. I had just related some of the research I'd read about the correlation between scrolling and its impacts. The research shows that endless scrolling on social media is correlated with heightened dopamine-driven reward cycles, reduced attention spans, and altered patterns of brain development in young people, making sustained focus and discernment more difficult.[9]

"What about neuroplasticity?" I asked.

"Nope. I've had conversations with Aquinas people [scholars who study Thomas Aquinas], and they say that at some point the spiritual senses, and there are a few of them, cannot withstand certain brain injury or atrophy."

I sipped my coffee and thought about his statements. Mark was still hopeful even as he maintained that young people would not have access to their spiritual senses if they didn't have them awakened before they reached adolescence. How did he maintain his positive outlook? I was the one, as a college professor, who interfaced with hundreds of students every year. He mostly worked with older intellectuals.

"If a whole generation of young people do not have a spiritual sense, in your view, how does this bode well for society?" I asked.

"Oh, it doesn't bode well in the immediate future," he said. "So, the Millennial Generation, and many, not all, of Generation Z, will have issues. But the Digital Sphere and its forms of social media have only just begun, and they will initiate memory, not fantasy. The youngest will be swimming in a completely different sea of information, and this is the change we need."

Mark describes the Digital Sphere, not as a new civilization, but as an autonomous psychotechnological entity. It possesses a sovereignty that is unprecedented and that supersedes nation-states and globalism, both of which are powerless to resist it.

Just as digital systems now mediate human perception, sacred architecture once mediated divine encounter. This brings us to the question of how environments shape the spiritual sense—not only through screens and code, but through material structures like stone or light, and senses like audio, or through silence. To understand what we are becoming under the digital regime, we must first recall what we once were—beings formed by cathedrals and nature, not circuits. The story of a young man's unexpected conversion in the cathedrals of Europe offers more than anecdote; it reveals a counterpoint to digital transcendence: an encounter not with simulation, but with presence.

THE ARCHITECTURE OF PRESENCE AND THE SPIRITUAL SENSE

A few years ago, I met a young priest who had told me about his conversion to Catholicism. He had been an atheist in college, and explained that he was a somewhat self-destructive young man. After he graduated, he decided to tour Europe on foot. Like most tourists, he visited the great cathedrals like France's Chartres and Notre-Dame de Paris. Unexpectedly, within these structures he felt a presence. He chalked up his experience to being particular to the one or two cathedrals he visited, but as he toured more of them he felt the same presence. He soon came to the belief that he was feeling the presence of God. His conversion was brought about by the architecture, the environment that held a certain presence. These environments awakened his spiritual sense.

Medieval Gothic architecture emerged around 1140 CE in the Île-de-France region, most notably with Abbot Suger's reconstruction of the Abbey Church of Saint-Denis. Originally known as *opus Francigenum* ("French work"), the term "Gothic" was later applied derisively during the Renaissance. Gothic architecture is characterized by pointed arches, ribbed vaults, and flying buttresses, which allowed for soaring vertical structures and vast stained glass windows. These features weren't merely structural innovations—they embodied a theological vision. For Abbot Suger and others influenced by Neoplatonic and Augustinian thought, light was a manifestation of the divine, and height symbolized the soul's ascent toward God.

Although never formally declared the church's official style, Gothic architecture became its de facto sacred form. The Catholic Church's growing influence helped spread the style across Europe. Its alignment with Christian theology—emphasizing transcendence, order, and divine illumination—made it the natural architecture for cathedrals and monastic spaces. By the thirteenth century, iconic cathedrals like Chartres, Notre-Dame, and Reims had cemented Gothic architecture as the visual and spiritual language of Latin Christendom. The young priest's story reminds us that architecture is not simply symbolic—it is a medium that influences and shapes us.

McLuhan helps us see that all media, not just sacred architecture, but books, screens, and algorithms, are environments. They are not passive containers of information, but active forces that reshape perception, behavior, and consciousness. For McLuhan, the algorithm is not immaterial; it has a materiality and a structure. It conditions us even when we don't see it. Like flying buttresses and vaulted ceilings, algorithms hold up our digital cathedrals—search engines, feeds, platforms—but in doing so, they reconfigure our inner lives.

The spiritual sense that once responded to light through stained glass now responds—if at all—to the unseen architectures of recommendation systems and machine learning algorithms. The question is not whether we are being formed, but how—and toward what end. According to Mark, that end must be religion.

"Programs are driving the bus," he said. "These superficial elements that ride on top of something else, that is the fundamental structure, and it is a psychotechnological structure. Computers are nothing but elaborate memory devices. If the computer gets its memory confused, nothing works. Computers are not alive, they don't have souls.

"The underlying architectural foundation which is the fundamental dimension of digital, and the one which humans really have no choice now but to grapple with. The best defense and way through is faculty psychology that started with Aristotle. Thomas Aquinas took it from there.

What we just lived through, the twentieth century, was an era of distorted imagination because imagination dominates the headlines. Utopian and Dystopian. The question was always: How do we escape this world? Fantasy ran the world, but it is now replaced by a world that runs on memory, because memory is the architecture of the reality upon which we live. We are in a transition from a fantasy world to a memory world.

"The characteristics of this new environment, which is based on memory and is driven by digital technologies, must be less work, because the robots will do the work, and more religion. Because humans are not going to be satisfied with a meaningless life."

The young priest felt the presence of God in the cathedrals because that architecture was designed to disclose it. Our digital environments also contain presence, but its source and meaning are obscure. Whether these architectures become vessels of revelation or engines of distortion depends on whether we cultivate the spiritual sense that can tell the difference.

8

A RIVAL STAR: PIERRE TEILHARD DE CHARDIN'S SCI-FI THEOLOGY

> Ever since my childhood an enigmatic force had been impelling me, apparently in conflict with the "Supernatural," towards some Ultra-human; and in trying to pin it down I had become accustomed to regard it as emanating not from God but from a rival Star.
>
> —Pierre Teilhard de Chardin, *The Heart of Matter*

In the early twentieth century, French Jesuit priest and paleontologist Pierre Teilhard de Chardin proposed a radical vision of humanity's future that was so strange it was met with suspicion, censure, and even scorn by the Catholic Church. Defying ecclesiastical suppression, Chardin described the human as being a vibrating, thinking mass that will form into a giant network of mind, matter, economic, and artistic forces and would ultimately station itself above Earth's biosphere. This conception of the human being was, and still is, so foreign to modern definitions of personhood—rooted in individualism, biology, and autonomy—that it offends the sensibilities of both religious orthodoxy and secular rationalism alike. Teilhard articulated this vision, the *noosphere* (from Greek *nous* (νοῦς), meaning "mind" or "intellect"), decades before Marshall McLuhan's media theories and Arthur C. Clarke's novels, anticipating a networked, planetary mind long before it entered public imagination.[1]

Chardin's life, language, and very bearing was steeped in a lived mysticism so far beyond ordinary experience that it virtually guaranteed his relegation to the margins of respectable society. His prose was strange to some, but familiar to those well versed in UFO experiencer literature—it often reads like a forerunner to that genre. His spiritual autobiography, *The Heart of Matter*, written five years before his death, is a blend of historical reflection and devotional writing. It traces the development of his spiritual perception or sense and is interspersed with prayers to Jesus Christ and visionary passages. These are framed, at times, in symbolic language drawn from what scholars refer to as the *Merkabah* tradition—a Jewish mystical lineage centered on the prophetic visions of divine chariots, especially those described in the Book of Ezekiel (notably "Ezekiel's wheel"). In this tradition, the *Merkabah* (Hebrew for "chariot") refers to the celestial object that carries the presence of God, and it became a central image in early Jewish mystical ascent literature and continues through early Christian and medieval monastic Christian sects. At the heart of this mysticism are angel contact events and lived mystical reality.

Though his ideas were once seen as radical and possibly heretical, Chardin's vision has, in the early twenty-first century, garnered renewed attention from both the upper echelons of the Catholic Church and a new generation of tech accelerationists. Pope Benedict XVI commended Chardin's vision of a "true cosmic liturgy . . . where the cosmos becomes a living host," and urged priests to see their role as consecrating the world itself[2]—a direct reference to Chardin's "The Mass on the World." Jesuit Fr. Federico Lombardi noted that Chardin was no longer considered heterodox (heretical) and could be openly studied. In his 2015 encyclical "Laudato Si'," Pope Francis cited Chardin by name and framed his vision of evolution and the noosphere as part of a theological and ecological journey toward unity. He also quoted Chardin's "The Mass on the World" during a homily, thus bringing Chardin's mystical cosmology into a global, pastoral context.

In *The Phenomenon of Man*, Chardin argued that humanity was not at the end of history, but "at the beginning of something new"[3]—a convergence of consciousness and complexity. Central to his vision was the emergence of the noosphere, the "thinking layer" of the Earth, formed through intensifying interconnection—scientific, technological, and spiritual. This planetary sheath of thought, he believed, would envelop the globe as humanity grew increasingly aware of its collective destiny: "Mankind, instead of working against itself, is beginning to work in concert."[4] Chardin did not see this as a traditional apocalypse, but as a moment of planetary transformation. In *The Future of Man*, he warns: "The age of nations is past. The task before us now, if we would not perish, is to build the earth."[5] His vision was not one of destruction, but of *Christogenesis*: the unification of all personal consciousness in a loving, divine center. He called this process the *Omega Point*.

It is difficult to imagine that Marshall McLuhan and Arthur C. Clarke were unaware of Chardin's writings; the thematic and conceptual parallels are too pronounced to be coincidental, even if neither author credits him, although, as I noted earlier, Clarke does elaborate on Chardin's ideas in a late publication. Mark Stahlman indicated that McLuhan had likely read mimeographed versions of Chardin's publications that had circulated privately. McLuhan's idea of the "electronic environment" as a medium for global cerebration closely resembles Chardin's noosphere—though stripped of its spiritual teleology. Likewise, Chardin's vision of humanity's evolutionary ascent bears an uncanny resemblance to Clarke's Overmind. Both depict a planetary awakening of consciousness, but with radically different moral valences. Clarke's Overmind entails the dissolution of the individual into a cold cosmic intelligence, while Chardin insists that true spiritual convergence preserves and magnifies the uniqueness of each person.

In "A Great Event Foreshadowed: The Planetization of Mankind," a chapter in *The Future of Man*, Chardin describes the formation of the new human linked to the noosphere. He states that humanity is going to experience itself enveloped in something that is like a thinking envelope that surrounds the Earth. It is not the biosphere, but a sphere beyond that which was already in development in his lifetime, and which he predicted was in his near future.[6]

Reading through Chardin's theology I was struck by how it operated as a kind of sacred science fiction. Around the time I was reviewing his work, I was invited to speak at a conference hosted at a renowned abbey, which also serves as the campus of an elite residential high school. The setting was stunning; tall pine trees framed the grounds, and winding trails opened onto a quiet beach along the Atlantic Ocean. The theme of the two-day gathering was "Digital Technology and the Catholic Church," and the participants included priests, monks, teachers, and parents, many of whom interact daily with the students who live and learn there. As the conversations unfolded, it became clear that few, if any, had ever heard of Pierre Teilhard de Chardin. While his vision of a spiritually charged, technologically evolving humanity was being quoted at the highest levels of the church, it had scarcely reached the institutional imagination of those tasked with guiding the next generation through the very terrain Chardin foresaw.

A highlight of the event was a mass held in the abbey's church, which was as breathtaking as the surrounding landscape. It was celebrated in the traditional form, complete with Gregorian chants, clouds of incense, and the Latin liturgy. After the mass the participants went to eat lunch in a large conference room. The organizers hoped to foster deep conversation, so they seated us at large round tables and provided thoughtful prompts to guide our discussions.

Just before we ate, the community's leader stood to offer a prayer on behalf of the two hundred gathered participants. This was a plea for wisdom, for clarity, but mostly for God's help in guiding the church through a time of the deep uncertainty brought about by AI. There was no pretense in his voice. In his words I heard a leader who felt adrift and perhaps unable to shepherd his flock. The sincerity of his invocation moved me. My talk was scheduled after lunch. I was seated with a student, her mother, a few donors, another professor who was also a featured speaker, and a priest who was an educator at the school as well as a member of the community.

One of the donors asked the group about the definition of AI. He wanted to know what it was, and who came up with the definition. The other professor, a friend of mine, provided a technical answer to the man's question and a robust conversation began about AI and its implications for the church. Someone mentioned the work of Chardin. I knew that his order, the Jesuit Order, had silenced him and forbade him to teach about this aspect of his work.

"Thankfully," I said, "his work is now being understood as prescient and relevant."

This sentence, the first I uttered at the table, prompted a swift reaction by the priest.

He craned his neck to look at me, his eyes squinting with scorn, and he blurted, "That's not true." Then he scoffed, "That's ridiculous."

I felt heat rise in my body and settle in my cheeks. This feeling, sadly, was familiar. It used to happen in some of my courses at the Jesuit School of Theology. For the most part I was accepted by my priest-professors as a student with valuable contributions. But occasionally a professor would cut me off or just not listen to me. I remember telling my father about these instances.

"Jesuits are trained to not see women," my father said. I figured he meant that they followed their vows in the strictest sense. He, too, was trained by Jesuits and had attended Catholic schools his whole life.

I continued my input at the table because I knew I wasn't wrong, even though my first inclination was to look up Chardin on my phone and make sure I was right. I quickly realized, *Of course I am right, I've been studying this for years.*

"Actually, his work was silenced by the church," I said. I assumed the priest would reconsider his position, but he didn't.

He looked at me again, as if he couldn't believe I had the gall to continue, and he laughed.

"What are you talking about? The church never did that."

He lifted his hand in a gesture of dismissal. I recognized him as the person who'd administered Communion at Mass.

After lunch we all took a break and everyone at the table got up to get coffee. I found myself alone and I decided to take a few moments to get ready for my talk. I sat quietly and began to rehearse my main points. My talk was about social media and its effects on young people. Before I could finish my reflection, a man reached for a chair and positioned it directly in front of me, an action that seemed deliberate. He looked directly into my eyes. This man, I surmised, was not a Catholic educator.

"I am here to observe the impact your talk makes on this audience," he began.

I listened and then briefly looked around. I wondered if I should alert someone, but the man didn't seem as if he were a potential threat, and there were two hundred people surrounding us.

He said he worked for a specific government agency. "There are a lot of people there who support what you're doing. We know about *the others*. What you're doing is brave."

I didn't have time to ask what he meant because my talk was about to begin, and the conference organizer was already motioning me toward the stage. Unsure of how to respond, I simply nodded.

"Thank you," I said. "I hope you enjoy the talk."

As I stepped up to the podium, I noticed he had moved to the edge of the room. He remained standing, watching the audience rather than me. I tried to focus on my words, but I couldn't shake the feeling that something strange was unfolding—something outside the boundaries of the visible script.

Later that evening, at the crowded reception, I saw that three organizers of the event were off in a corner of the hall and had encircled the man. It looked as if they were interrogating him. My professor friend, who was one of the three, later sent me a text message and asked me if I knew the man. I did not.

"I think he's the real deal," I replied. The man had shown me his card and there were other indications that he was who he said he was.

After my talk, the mother who had been sitting next to me mentioned the man's sweatshirt and asked him about it. She recognized it because her brother also worked for that agency. The man seemed uncomfortable after being identified.

Although the circumstances of the man's presence were strange, he proved to be a wonderful conversationalist. He was knowledgeable about the history of esotericism, traditions that allegedly passed along secret knowledge. He had made reference to "the others" earlier, just to me, and I knew or strongly suspected that he was referencing the UFO phenomena and nonhuman intelligence. I didn't bring that up in the conversation at the table. He had mentioned that others in his organization knew my work. I felt like the man was a friend.

Later that night, as the ocean winds moved through the pines and the abbey lights flickered against the dark, I kept thinking about the man's words. I felt that he had brought a wave of invisible support. The encounter with the man might have been strange, but what disturbed me more than the man's badge or the implications of surveillance was the church's and most of the speakers' palpable uncertainty in the face of what AI represents, which was made obvious throughout the conference. This wasn't just a crisis of ethics or policy—it was a sense of being spiritually unmoored. And yet, Pierre Teilhard de Chardin had seen this coming. Long before neural networks and brain-machine interfaces, he saw the world moving toward a new form of consciousness—a convergence he called *ultra-hominization*. Like McLuhan and Clarke, he foresaw a new human being, which he named the *Ultra-human*.

CHARDIN'S SPIRITUAL SENSE

At lunch, when Chardin's name surfaced during a conversation about AI and the church, I realized just how contested his legacy still is. What struck me was not just the priest's ignorance of Chardin and the church's suppression of his work, but the deep anxiety running beneath the surface—an anxiety about whether the future taking shape through our technologies could still be held within a theological frame. Within the context of McLuhan's supraterrestrial, and Clarke's Overmind, Chardin's Ultra-human pushes the limits of hope and despair.

As a trained paleontologist and scientist, Chardin sought to reconcile materiality with spirituality. He lived at a time when evolutionary theory and Catholic doctrine seemed irreconcilable, yet he insisted that evolution was not a threat to faith but its culmination. To him, matter was not opposed to spirit; it was spirit in the process of becoming. The cosmos was unfolding toward a point of ultimate convergence—not into an impersonal force like Clarke's Overmind, but into a radiant center of love and intelligence that Chardin called the Omega Point: Christ at the end of evolution. During his life, he was silenced by church authorities and his major theological works were published only posthumously. The force of his character and theories, however, made an unforgettable impression on scientists, scholars, and intellectuals during his lifetime. He argued that both matter and evolution are spiritualized because spirit is latent in matter and becomes more conscious through evolution.[7]

Just as McLuhan identified the spiritual sense as something as real as hearing or sight, so did Chardin. He felt it as a child and described how it evolved and changed throughout his life. He described it as an interior sense and associated it with a feeling of "plentitude." It consists of a "particular psychological disposition" and is "certainly common to all men (although not always formally recognized by them) and for want of a better name I shall call it the Sense of Plentitude."[8]

This sense "belongs to a higher order and contains them all."[9] Throughout Chardin's life he described its development as involving several spiritual senses that are related to one another. The development of these senses is the most important thread of his work and it grounds his life's mission. "Everything that follows will be simply the story of a slow unfolding or evolving within me of this fundamental and 'Protean' element which takes on ever richer and purer forms."[10]

Significantly, he insists that the recognition of this sense began when he was six years old as he contemplated what he found to be the most enduring material, a chunk of iron.

The young Chardin was attracted to this particular chunk of iron because it represented something that appeared eternal to him. It was so solid that he couldn't conceive of it ceasing to exist. However, as he grew up, it soon became apparent to him that his large block of iron was subject to rust and therefore decay. He replaced the iron with quartz, and this began his career as a budding scientist of material culture and eventually paleontology. His spiritual sense was further developed at other times in his life. In each instance he felt the spiritual sense physically, as material and ontological—that is, grounded in the nature of material reality itself. After studying theology at a college in Hastings, England he wrote that he felt "a presence much more than as an abstract notion, the consciousness of a deep-running, ontological, total Current which embraced the whole Universe in which I moved; and this consciousness continued to grow until it filled the whole horizon of my inner being."[11]

This feeling, which he identified as spiritual *and* physical, compelled him to reassess the dualism of spirit and matter, which he assumed was an axiom or even the basis of Christianity. Because his research apparently challenged what he thought was a dogma of the church, he became alarmed. He came to believe that, instead, "Matter and Spirit: these were no longer two things, but two states or two aspects of one and the same cosmic Stuff."[12]

Dualism posits that matter as inferior or fallen, and spirit as the sole locus of salvation, and it is a common idea in which many Christians believe. Chardin saw that his research posed a profound challenge to this assumption. Yet, from a doctrinal standpoint, Catholicism is not inherently dualistic. The idea of the incarnation itself proclaims the union of divine and material natures, and patristic and Thomistic thought (Aquinas) affirm that matter is good, that the body will be resurrected, and that grace builds on nature—not bypassing or negating it. Chardin's work actually revitalized these early Christian ideas in light of modern cosmology and evolutionary theory. He saw spiritual ascent as emerging from within the evolutionary process, not in rejection of it.

His mystical experiences led him to believe that evolution was directed by an intelligence, and that this intelligence could be observed in matter through processes of evolution. While on the front of World War I, his spiritual sense revealed the direct connection to the network of human consciousness he would later term the noosphere:

> The atmosphere of "the Front": it was, I am quite sure, from having plunged into that atmosphere—from having been soaked in it for months and months on end—and precisely where it was at its most dense and heavily charged, that I ceased to notice any break (if not any difference) between "physical" and "moral." . . . I have no doubt at all (as I said earlier) that it was the experience of the War that brought me this awareness and developed it in me as *a sixth sense.*
>
> Once I had acquired this complementary sense, what emerged into my field of perception was literally a new Universe.[13]

McLuhan described how his own spiritual sense was as obvious to him as seeing a physical object was for another, and similarly Chardin is surprised that others don't share his vision. His use of the word "astonished" is usually reserved for how he feels about how others do not share these perceptions.

"I was later to be astonished on many occasions to find in my own circle that those who could not agree with me suffered from a complete inability to understand. . . . This gift or faculty of perceiving, without actually seeing, the reality and organicity of collective magnitude is still comparatively rare."[14]

In later footnotes, he believes that this faculty of perception "will rapidly become general in the makeup of future generations."[15]

This new universe, perceived through his spiritual or "sixth sense," was not only moral and mystical—it was spatial and material. He saw an emergent stratum of reality composed of human consciousness itself, and he began to understand humanity as forming a planetary membrane—a sheath of interrelated thought, action, and intentionality—that encircled the Earth. The term *the noosphere* was likely first coined by the Russian geochemist Vladimir Vernadsky, who thought of it as the third stage of Earth's development, following the geosphere and biosphere, and shaped by the impact of human reason and activity. Chardin believed that he perceived it directly. He also believed that it represented an evolutionary leap—a new planetary layer where human consciousness and spiritual convergence shape the future of the Earth. And, he believed that people would soon develop the spiritual sense to perceive this as well.

CLARKE AND CHARDIN: FURTHER REFLECTIONS

Chardin and Arthur C. Clarke describe, with uncanny similarity, a planetary future in which human consciousness transcends its biological and national boundaries. Chardin, writing from within the Catholic tradition, frames this convergence as the Omega Point—a spiritual attractor drawing all life into union with the divine, where each person is transfigured yet retains their singularity. Decades later, Clarke imagines a similar outcome: Humanity's children evolve into a higher intelligence that merges with the Overmind, an immense alien consciousness. Clarke's vision is starkly disenchanted and antireligious. The children no longer resemble humans. Their absorption marks the end of the species, rather than its fulfillment.

Chardin's vision is theological, grounded in mysticism. He believed the Earth is developing a noosphere, a membrane of collective thought and intentionality, shaped by spiritual and technological forces alike. For him, evolution is not random but directional—toward more complexity, more interiority, and ultimately toward God. Chardin argued that spiritual convergence intensifies rather than erases the uniqueness of each person. Clarke, by contrast, offers a kind of secular rapture. His evolved humanity vanishes into a radiant intelligence that is cosmic, but characterized as unkempt and unified in their indifference.

Where Chardin sees the sacred—for him, Christ—at the summit of consciousness, Clarke sees an impersonal and final end to humanity. Clarke's novel portrays the end of human beings, while Chardin prophesizes human transfiguration, the resurrected human of Christian revelation.

Both Clarke and Chardin envision evolution as a process ending in union—but their destinations, while structurally similar, are theologically opposed. Clarke's Overmind represents the final stage of consciousness: a supraindividual intelligence that absorbs humanity, dissolving the self in a seamless collective. Chardin's Omega Point, by contrast, is not impersonal but profoundly incarnational: Christ at the apex of all evolution, where each person is perfected, not erased. For both thinkers, consciousness is the axis of ascent—Clarke imagines telepathy, precognition, and hive mind as evolutionary thresholds; Chardin moves from matter to life through his spiritual senses. Each reinterprets religion through the lens of science: Clarke strips it to its contact mechanics—mystical experiences as misunderstood interfaces with advanced intelligences—while Chardin transfigures Christianity itself into a cosmic process, with the figure of Christ anchoring the arc of time, biology, and soul.

Where they diverge is just as revealing as where they align. Clarke's Overmind is vast, intelligent, and utterly impersonal. It absorbs humanity without recognizing the individual, offering no memory, no love, no redemption. In theological terms, it reads as post-human—a vision of transcendence stripped of grace. Chardin's Omega Point, by contrast, is radically personal and centered in divine love. For him, union with the divine does not erase personhood; it intensifies it. Clarke's telos is technological: The Overlords guide humanity's ascent through tools and science. Chardin's is theological: While technology participates in the process, it is merely the scaffolding for a spiritual ascent driven by love, awareness, and sacred purpose.

CHARDIN'S NOOSPHERE IN SILICON VALLEY AND AUSTIN

Fast-forward to Austin, 2024, at the South by Southwest Conference. My Uber driver explains that many of the technopreneurs of Silicon Valley have relocated here. In a renovated warehouse I attend the demonstration of a large-scale "engine"—an AI trained on billions of social posts to illustrate, with music and graphics, whatever you prompt it to. What caught my attention was not the product itself but the language the lead engineer used to describe their endgame: "We're mapping the noosphere in real time." She said it without irony, and I wasn't sure if she was fully aware of the theological provenance.

The church once silenced Chardin for conflating salvation and evolution, yet tech entrepreneurs now canonize him precisely for that conflation. Many of today's AI leaders and thinkers, intentionally or not, invoke Chardin's vision of the noosphere. In the business world, a recent *Forbes* article, "Is AI Taking Us to the Heart of the Noosphere?," directly draws this parallel, proposing that the rise of AI may mark the transition into a "living noosphere," where human and machine consciousness coevolve.[16]

Other observers go further. The *NonZero Newsletter*, reflecting on Jaron Lanier's insights, calls ChatGPT "a brain of brains"[17]—a formulation that echoes Chardin's own language for the noosphere. This idea—that AI systems weave together distributed human insight into a higher-order cognitive structure—would not surprise Chardin. Scholars and commentators alike are recognizing that we're approaching something like his "thinking envelope of the Earth," even if they use different metaphors. Publications like *Kosmos Journal* now proclaim "The Noosphere Is Here," suggesting that Chardin's once-esoteric theology is rapidly becoming a framework for understanding the present.

We are now undeniably in the era of the noosphere—not as a speculative future, but as a present reality. What Chardin once envisioned as a shimmering horizon of collective thought and spiritual evolution has become, for many, the baseline condition of our digital lives. Did Chardin believe, like Clarke's novel suggests and McLuhan predicts, the arrival of a new form of human being? It appears so.

Chardin believed that the noosphere would prepare the way for the emergence of a new human—what he called the *Ultra-human*. This was no mere enhancement of cognitive capacity or processing speed. It was the spiritual intensification of the person, oriented toward divine love. For Chardin, the Ultra-human is a transfigured form of the human being, not the post-human self. Christ stood at the end of the evolutionary arc not as an impersonal force, but as the radiant heart of the world, summoning all creation into union without erasure.

But today, AI technologists who speak of "mapping the noosphere" often mean something else. For some, the noosphere is not a spiritual horizon but a computational one. It is not a field of love, but of data. The new human being they envision is less a transfigured self than a brain-machine interface. Perhaps both are possible now.

So, we must ask: Are we building toward Chardin's Omega Point—or merely a neural net masquerading as one? Are we shaping technologies that help us become more fully human, or more easily replaced? Are both scenarios the case?

One thing is certain, and that is Chardin believed that the beginning of a new human being, a new form of human, was on his horizon. This is the Ultra-human. It is a new form of human being, and its existence, as well as human beings' existence, is not assured.

9

THE ULTRA-HUMAN AND THE TRANSFIGURED BODY

It is sown a physical body, it is raised a spiritual body.

—1 Cor. 15:44

The Mystical Body of Christ should, in fact, be conceived as a physical reality, in the strongest sense the words can bear. Only so can the great mysteries and the great virtues of religion . . . assume their full significance.

—Pierre Teilhard de Chardin, *Writings in Time of War*

I'm often invited to speak before church congregations, rooms filled with sincere people navigating the mysteries of their faith. There is one biblical passage, more than any other, that has always confounded me, for good reason. It describes an event that is hard to square with contemporary theories of the human body. It comes from the Gospel of Matthew (27:50–54), and is a scene as strange as it is overlooked. At the moment of Jesus's death, the earth quakes, the veil of the temple tears, and then something utterly astonishing transpires: Tombs split open, and the dead, described as "holy ones," rise and walk into Jerusalem, appearing to many. It is a moment that parallels, even foreshadows, the resurrection of Christ himself. And yet, despite its narrative force, this episode is rarely taught and almost never preached. When mentioned at all, it is typically dismissed as a theological flourish or interpreted symbolically. But for modern readers, and scholars like me, it confronts us with a disturbing possibility: Did the Gospel writers mean this literally? What if bodies really did rise? And what, then, are we to make of our own?

> And Jesus cried out again with a loud voice, and yielded up His spirit. Then, behold, the veil of the temple was torn in two from top to bottom; and the earth quaked, and the rocks were split, and the graves were opened; and many bodies of the saints who had fallen asleep were raised; and coming out of the graves after His resurrection, they went into the holy city and appeared to many. So when the centurion and those with him, who were guarding Jesus, saw the earthquake and the things that had happened, they feared greatly, saying, "Truly this was the Son of God!"[1]

Faithful Christians do not easily dismiss passages from the New Testament, especially those that seem strange and unsettling. Did people literally rise from their tombs, physically, and then walk into the city to show themselves? How did the onlookers react? Was this truly just a rhetorical device to emphasize the absolute novelty of the Christian message? The truth was, I never had a definitive interpretation of this passage, so I often turned to description: I cited the relevant sources and outlined how theologians throughout history have interpreted them, and left it up to my audience to form their own conclusions. That was the best I could do. I had not yet plumbed the depths of Chardin's notion of the glorified body and his reading of the Apostle Paul's *pneumatikon sōma*, the material body animated by God's spirit. Was Paul speaking metaphorically, or literally? Chardin, it's now clear to me, believed Paul was describing something embodied, something ontological. He believed that Paul was not using poetic language, but describing a new kind of human existence. Chardin's vision gave this strange passage in Matthew a renewed plausibility.

Today, the idea of a "new human" is no longer confined to scripture or mystical theology. It has migrated into the language of venture capital, neuroscience, and artificial intelligence. In Austin and Silicon Valley, and at conferences and in labs, talk of human enhancement, whether through brain-machine interfaces, synthetic biology, or consciousness upload, echoes, perhaps unwittingly, the eschatological tones of early Christianity. But this "post-human" vision often lacks what Paul and Chardin considered essential: a moral and spiritual transformation, or transfiguration. Where Chardin spoke of the *pneumatikon sōma*—a body spiritualized through love and moral effort—for the most part, technologists envision a body optimized for efficiency and longevity. According to Paul's vision, only certain bodies will inherit the future. In Chardin's universe, the Ultra-human body is the future.

THE APOSTLE PAUL AND THE RESURRECTED BODY

A Christian man, now known as the Apostle Paul, stands at the crossroads of Jewish tradition and the emergent Christian movement in the first century. Born Saul, he was a Roman citizen in Tarsus and trained as a Pharisee formed by the traditions of Second Temple Judaism, the form of Jewish religious life and thought that developed after the return from Babylonian exile (circa 516 BCE) and lasted until the destruction of the Second Temple in 70 CE. This was a period rich in theological development, with competing interpretations of the law, the coming of a messiah, the resurrection of the dead, and the end of the world. Paul, as a Pharisee, belonged to a group that believed in the resurrection and the eventual renewal of creation—ideas that would later become central to his Christian theology. Before this, however, he persecuted Christians, as a Pharisee and a citizen of Rome who did not believe that Jesus was the Jewish messiah.

Paul was fluent in Greek philosophical discourse, and literate in Roman jurisprudence. His genuine letters, the earliest texts in the New Testament corpus, do not merely shape Christian doctrine, they form its foundation and constitute almost one-third of the New Testament. Paul's conversion to Christianity didn't arise from just theoretical speculation, like Girard's or McLuhan's, but from a personal encounter. Paul had a visionary experience on the road to the town of Damascus, where he had planned to prosecute and potentially kill Christians. Described in Acts 9, Acts 22, and

Acts 26, and referenced in Paul's own letters (notably Galatians 1:15–16 and 1 Corinthians 15:8), an event occurred on the road to Damascus, where Paul (then known as Saul) is enveloped by a blinding light and hears a voice. He believes he has met the risen Christ.

This event leaves Paul temporarily blinded and transformed. He believes he has had a real encounter with Jesus's transfigured body. Because of this, he places himself among those to whom the resurrected Christ appeared, equating his encounter with the post-resurrection appearances to Peter, the Twelve, and others. He identifies himself as an apostle. For Paul, this moment was not only revelatory—it was also vocational: It marked his divine commissioning as Apostle to the Gentiles and laid the foundation for his theology of resurrection and bodily transformation. He changes his name from Saul to Paul to indicate that he has become a new man.

Paul's writings suggest he believed in a material, tangible transformation of human bodies in the eschaton, or the end times. End time theology, or eschatology—study of the end times—is a very diverse array of beliefs that are unique to different Christian denominations. Catholics believe that the end times happened in the first century after Jesus was resurrected. They are waiting for his next coming. Other Christian denominations believe in dispensational millenarianism, where there will be a physical rapture of the elect who will rise and meet Jesus when he comes again. Paul describes a spiritual body in 1 Corinthians 15:50 that implies that the resurrection is a material metamorphosis. "Flesh and blood cannot inherit the kingdom of God," he writes. Instead, a new kind of body—a transfigured body that is destined for those incorporated into what he calls the *sōma Christou*, the Mystical Body of Christ. Does this reference to a body of flesh and blood indicate that the body that will inherit the kingdom of God is purely spiritual, that is, nonmaterial? I used to think so, and this is the dualism against which Chardin struggled. Paul likely meant something entirely different.

Paul was martyred in Rome; according to tradition he was beheaded under Emperor Nero, likely around the same time that the Apostle Peter was said to have been crucified upside down. Their willingness to face such brutal deaths suggests they were convinced that death was not an end but a beginning. Paul and Peter believed they encountered Jesus in a bodily, though transfigured, form, and this would have been profoundly persuasive.

While Paul's notion of the body is not easily understood by contemporary Christians, scholars like Dale Martin, author of *The Corinthian Body*, place Paul's theology of the body within the context of Greco-Roman medical and philosophical thought, rather than later Christian ideas that inherited dualist assumptions from modern philosophy, and with which Chardin struggled.

Martin argues that Paul's idea of the resurrected body is not a contradiction in terms but reflects an ancient understanding of different types of physical bodies. In the ancient world, "spiritual" didn't mean "nonphysical"—it referred to a finer, more glorious, more divine kind of body. Spirit was not immaterial, but a different form of matter.

Martin writes that ancient Greek physiological categories posited a "hierarchy of substances": at the top were pure, fiery, airy, subtle forms of matter (like stars or gods), and at the bottom were heavy, coarse, decaying materials. Paul's spiritual body (1 Cor 15:44) belongs to the higher end of this continuum. It's still a body, but it is no longer corruptible or tied to fleshly passions. Martin argues that modern interpreters have misread Paul by assuming that "spiritual" must mean nonmaterial. That's a modern dualism, not Paul's. Paul was not rejecting the body or advocating for disembodied souls. Rather, he was offering a vision of bodily transformation, rooted in ancient understandings of graded materiality.

This type of body was immortal. One could achieve the transfigured body through one's actions and internal focus on Jesus. Paul's experience of the resurrected Jesus provided him with the will to do what normal people would avoid. As a new Christian, Paul was constantly in danger. "On frequent journeys, [I was] in danger from rivers, danger from robbers, danger from my own people, danger from Gentiles, danger in the city, danger in the wilderness, danger at sea, danger from false brothers."[2] Why did he put himself in danger? He did this because he had experienced love from Jesus. "Who shall separate us from the love of Christ? Shall trouble or hardship or persecution or famine or nakedness or danger or sword?[3] The danger couldn't compete with the experience of being a part of the Mystical Body. Not only that, but after his experience of seeing the transfigured Christ, he experienced a shift in his will. According to Thomas Aquinas, the will (*Voluntas*) is part of the spiritual sense.

When Paul wasn't in danger, he was in jail. Making the most of his incarceration, he wrote letters to the various early Christian communities whose members were not, in his view, adequately prepared for the end times. He directed them to practice virtues to ensure that they achieved their transfigured bodies. To the Philippians, he wrote: "But our citizenship is in heaven. And we eagerly await a Savior from there, the Lord Jesus Christ, who, by the power that enables him to bring everything under his control, will transform our lowly bodies so that they will be like his glorious body."[4]

CHARDIN'S CLARIFICATION OF PAUL'S RESURRECTED BODY

Chardin, writing nearly two thousand years after Paul, carries Paul's vision forward and into the era of evolution and the technological transformation of consciousness. For Chardin, the glorified body is not passively received at death. It is built, just as Paul taught, through actions, intentions, and ethical labor in the world. These interior qualities have consequential effects for material bodies. Chardin's work can be read as a response to Paul's question: "With what kind of body do they come?"[5] Chardin describes the transfigured body and instructs in its construction.

"By grace, Jesus Christ is united to all sanctified souls, and since the bonds that link souls to him in one single hallowed mass end in Him and meet in Him, and hold together by Him, it is He who reigns and He who lives; the whole body is His in its entirety. Souls, however, are not a group of isolated monads. As the 'cosmic view' specifically shows us, they make up one single whole with the universe, consolidated by life and matter. Christ."[6]

To have a glorified body is to be incorporated into a "mass" networked consciousness, not like the internet, but a sanctified group. It is sanctified because it contains internal gatekeepers—acts of goodness that have become known as the virtues. One enters the gates either as a gift from God (grace), or through practicing virtuous actions, often without worldly reward.

> Our efforts . . . build up a Body in the true sense of the word. This is the Body of Christ, which seeks to be realized in each one of us.
>
> Our efforts have an impact that is far more permanent and profound. . . . When our activity is animated by grace it is as effective and "creative" as life, the Mother of Organisms, and it builds up a Body in the true sense of the word. This is the Body of Christ, which seeks to be realized in each one of us.[7]

Chardin extends St. Paul's doctrine of the glorified body—not as metaphor, but as a real transformation that fuses matter and spirit. For both thinkers, resurrection is not a metaphor for survival or hope. It is the fulfillment of the material world. St. Paul speaks of the *pneumatikon sōma*, the spiritual body, in 1 Corinthians 15. Chardin takes up this vision and expands it through the lens of evolution, proposing that we do not simply receive a glorified body—we participate in its construction through love, suffering, and action.

Chardin also warns modern Christians to resist easy metaphorical interpretations of the Mystical Body, and the transfigured body, as they appear in the New Testament. The transfigured body will absolutely appear *alien*. One should not be afraid of it, however.

> Minds that are afraid of a bold concept or are governed by individualistic prejudices, and always try to interpret the relationships between beings in moral or logical terms, are apt to conceive the Body of Christ by analogy with human associations; it then becomes much more akin to a social aggregation than to a natural organism. Such minds dangerously weaken the thought of Scripture and make it unintelligible or platitudinous to thinking men who are eager to trace out physical connections and relations that are specifically cosmic. They un-justifiably diminish Christ and the profoundly real mystery of his Flesh. The Body of Christ is not, as some unenterprising thinkers would have us believe, the extrinsic or juridical association of men who are embraced by one and the same benevolence and are destined to the same reward. It must be understood with boldness, as St John and St Paul and the Fathers saw it and loved it. It constitutes a world that is natural and new, an organism that is animate and in motion, one in which we are all united, physically and biologically.[8]

For Chardin, the danger is in viewing the church, or the Body of Christ, as an association that people join because they follow rules and agree to certain principles. This diminishes the reality. He believes that the church is a living organism, thus the language of the Body of Christ. It is a living thing as real as anything biological.

THE MORAL FACTOR

Chardin's project emphasizes the fusion of the moral with the material. It is significant, he argues, that Jesus, who is God, was born as a human being. The incarnation is not just about Jesus, but about matter in general. He believes that this foundational concept is revealed through time. His vision was of a future that, for him, was not too far off. The corporate body he foresaw appeared to be more than just a networked body, as McLuhan and Clarke foretold, but a networked mass made possible by moral intentions.

> It is, nevertheless, essential to the precision of our work and the delight we take in it, that we should try to define more exactly some of the factors responsible for this coincidence and some of the lines along which it runs. We must find out what can be the absolute residual elements in the cosmos which are destined to be incorporated in the celestial edifice; in what way the segregation of the elect into a hallowed mass may be influenced by the discoveries of pure science, of physics or history; and how, apart from the growth of supernatural merits, Christ is realized in Evolution.[9]

This is a type of salvation that includes science. Chardin suggests that the *formation of the Mystical Body* is created and shaped partly by knowledge, technology, and collective self-understanding. The glorified body is the end—not of an individualistic, escapist rapture—but of an *entire process of cosmic convergence*. Christ is both the initiator and the *fulfillment* of evolutionary becoming.

The Ultra-human, which is what is described, is the "third nature": after human nature comes a cosmic, risen nature—Christ as an evolutionary being. Chardin grapples with a painful paradox: Christian theology insists that spiritual progress hinges not on outward success but on inward intention. That is, even if our worldly projects fail, we can still be spiritually transformed—perhaps even more profoundly. This is consoling on one level, but deeply disorienting on another. It suggests that the actual success or failure of our material actions, their "cosmic quality," may be irrelevant to God. That notion, he admits, is "shocking to the unbeliever,"[10] and even troubling to faithful Christians.

Why? Because it seems to divide spiritual sanctification from the meaningfulness of our work in the world. What happens, Chardin asks, when the human mind—naturally drawn to coherence, integration, and progress—encounters a theological framework that appears to devalue earthly accomplishment? Christianity affirms the sanctity of sacrifice, suffering, and failure, but Chardin insists that this cannot mean rejecting the entire evolutionary impulse of creation itself. Christ condemned the world, but only the world of self-indulgence, not the world of effort, discipline, and creative striving. Nor of beauty, as when he asks us to consider the lilies of the field, we are told, "Not even Solomon in all of his glory was clothed like one of these."[11]

Chardin holds fast to the idea that cosmos itself carries a "mysterious promise of the future,"[12] embedded in its very structure. He acknowledges the anguish of the thinking Christian who cannot reconcile spiritual detachment with a love for the world's beauty, richness, and future. But he refuses to abandon the belief that our noble earthly labors, when aligned with a divine intention, can and must contribute to the building of the kingdom, not in spite of their materiality, but precisely through it.

THE THIRD NATURE: FROM HUMAN TO ULTRA-HUMAN

Chardin sees Christ not only as redeemer, but as the Evolver, the one in whom humanity finds its final form. He proposes a third nature beyond animal and rational nature: a cosmic or glorified nature in Christ. The glorified body, in this frame, is not merely a postmortem phenomenon, but the evolutionary destiny of all matter. This is what Chardin calls *Christogenesis*.

Chardin frames resurrection as a trajectory, not an event. It is not a reversal of death but the intensification of life—life that passes through death into transformed being. Morality is inextricable from materiality with respect to the transfigured body:

"The fundamental principle in the building up of the Body of Christ is making use of the subjective moral value of human acts. In the domain of morality the Divine and the Terrestrial meet and are fused into one."[13]

Chardin reflects on a paradox at the heart of Christian teaching. He emphasizes that in building the Body of Christ it is important to focus on the intention behind our actions, our sincerity, our goodwill, and our desire to do right. Even when one fails outwardly, one's efforts still matter spiritually. If one's intention is good, then every act, even a small or failed one, can contribute to the redemption of the world. That's because one's inner moral choices are the channel through which God's grace operates.

But there's a catch. Chardin sees a danger in this overemphasis on interior goodness: If the outward result doesn't matter, why strive for excellence? Where will our passion for truth and progress come from if the material world is spiritually secondary? He fears that this attitude could encourage complacency or detachment from real-world outcomes.

He illustrates this with the Christian view of suffering. Christianity often sees failure and suffering not just as unfortunate, but as spiritually beneficial—because they mirror Christ's own path of self-sacrifice. This path is central to Christian life: Growth often comes through loss, detachment, and pain—the "way of the Cross."

So, Chardin says, revelation (God's revealed truth) offers us a transformed future—a divine world born from the ashes of the old. But this also means that many of our deepest human hopes (for worldly success, mastery, or certainty) are frustrated or even labeled as spiritually dangerous. The kingdom of God grows alongside, and even in contradiction to, our visible, material progress.

THE NOOSPHERE AND THE ULTRA-HUMAN

Chardin's idea of the noosphere, the thinking envelope of the Earth, is directly tied to the resurrected body. The noosphere is not merely a realm of ideas. It is the embryonic form of a new kind of collective being. If the biosphere birthed the rational human, the noosphere births the transfigured one. When technopreneurs refer to the noosphere, they are generally not referencing morality as part of its fabric. Some envision the "post-human" as a purely computational being, liberated from biology. Others predict the rise of a "superintelligence" that will absorb or overwrite the human altogether. But this is not Chardin's Ultra-human.

Whereas Clarke's post-human visions often involve the erasure of the self, Chardin, like Paul, insists on the preservation and intensification of personhood. Just as Paul insists that the risen body is glorified (1 Cor. 15:43), Chardin believes the individual would not disappear in divine union but become more truly itself, radiant and connected.

Chardin's reading of Paul reveals a deeply evolutionary vision of the human person. For him, Paul was not merely a theologian, but a prophet of cosmic anthropology, a thinker who understood that the resurrected body was not a rejection of matter, but its perfection. In this view, the risen Christ is not simply a religious symbol but the *first fruit* of a long evolutionary process, one that culminates in spirit-infused matter. Matter is not discarded but transfigured. All of creation, according to Chardin's interpretation of Paul, is being drawn forward—radiantly—toward its fulfillment in Christ. The Ultra-human is the next iteration of the human being, the human being who succeeds.

THE PROPHET ELIJAH'S DESERT ENCOUNTER

> The man was walking in the desert, followed by his companion, when the Thing swooped down upon him.
>
> —PIERRE TEILHARD DE CHARDIN, *THE HEART OF MATTER*

One of the most curious passages in *The Heart of Matter* is Chardin's meditation on the "spiritual power of matter," which is appended in the book and is framed by the vision of the Hebrew prophet Elijah's fiery ascent (2 Kgs 2). In Jewish mystical tradition, this ascent is not merely a colorful story, but it is a foundation of the *Merkabah* ("chariot") literature. As noted in prior chapters, this tradition is an early form of Jewish mystical ascent centered on the prophet Ezekiel's vision of the divine throne borne by wheels and angelic beings (Ezek. 1). In this literature, often called *Hekhalot* mysticism, the adept seeks to ascend through the heavenly palaces to behold the enthroned glory of God. The journey was imagined as perilous: guarded by angelic gatekeepers, encircled by fiery hosts, and marked by the risk of madness or destruction for the unworthy. To engage the Merkabah, or chariot, was to attempt an ecstatic participation in the prophet Elijah's fiery ascent, but one undertaken with the knowledge that the heavenly realms could overwhelm or consume the visionary, sometimes by fire.

Anyone familiar with ufology will recognize the chariot tradition as being relevant to modern alien abduction and experiencer narratives. In both, a human is suddenly transported, often by a radiant vehicle, into another realm where they encounter beings of immense power and risk transformation or annihilation. David Halperin, a historian of Jewish mysticism who has written extensively on UFOs, has highlighted how Ezekiel's throne-chariot vision functions as an ancient analogue of modern "close encounters," with the fiery wheels and otherworldly beings prefiguring contemporary descriptions of spacecraft and their occupants. Others, such as Carl Raschke and Jeffrey Kripal, have also noted how the language of ascent mysticism and visionary transport shades seamlessly into the phenomenology of UFO contact.[14] In this light, Chardin's use of Elijah's fiery chariot to frame his "spiritual power of matter" situates his cosmology not only within Jewish mystical ascent traditions, but also within the same symbolic repertoire that underlies modern abduction testimony.

There are still other connections with modern ufology. Physicists and scientists tasked with attempting to crack the code of the apparently impossible technology of UFOs focus on their disregard of the laws of modernist physics. UFOs appear to be physical craft but defy gravity, appear and disappear, and in some cases are said to abduct human bodies. In this sense, experiencers report being transported through physical objects like walls and ceilings, and then returned physically to their homes, beds, or cars. Chardin places this passage within a section where he struggles with the nonduality of matter.

Chardin wrote the passage five years prior to his death in 1955. He not only places it within his autobiography, but he also elaborates on it in prose and poetry and ends the section in the book with a prayer to Jesus. It's an interesting passage, as it includes several themes: the taking up of a man, Elijah, to heaven, and thus bypassing death; the means of this abduction is a fiery chariot, which he calls "the Thing"; and the context, which was the death of Chardin's beloved friend who had been killed in World War I. He also references this friend's mystical pantheism as being significant.

Could Chardin be comparing his friend to Elijah? His interpretive revision of the passage suggests that Elijah, after having contact with the Thing, becomes a person who is no longer understood by men, and his body is also different from normal human beings. The chariot (as the Thing), separates, with some violence, Elijah from his friend. In Chardin's elaboration of Elijah's point of view, he paints him as being misunderstood precisely because his mysticism separates him from normal people. Elijah is assumed into heaven without passing from life to death. Recall that in the New Testament, Elijah appears with Jesus and Moses at Jesus's transfiguration, as described in three of the Gospels, which emphasizes that Chardin is referencing the transfigured body.

Chardin begins this section with the biblical passage 2 Kings 2:11.

"And as they went on walking and talking together,

behold a fiery chariot and fiery horses parted them both asunder; and of a sudden Elijah was caught up by a whirlwind into heaven."

Chardin writes from the point of view of Elijah:

> From afar it had appeared to him, quite small, gliding over the sand, no bigger than the palm of a child's hand—as a pale, fleeting shadow like a wavering flight of quail over the blue sea before sunrise or a cloud of gnats dancing in the sun at evening or a whirlwind of dust at midday sweeping over the plain.
>
> The Thing seemed to take no heed of the two travelers, and was roaming capriciously through the wilderness. Then, suddenly, it assumed a set course and with the speed of an arrow came straight at them.
>
> And then the man perceived that the little pale cloud of vapour was but the centre of an infinitely greater reality moving towards them without restriction, formless, boundless. The Thing as it approached them spread outwards with prodigious rapidity as far as his eyes could reach, filling the whole space, while its feet brushed lightly over the thorny vegetation beside the torrent, its brow rose in the sky like a golden mist with the reddening sun behind it. And all about it the ether had become alive, vibrating palpably.[15]

The man in Chardin's elaboration engages in a struggle with the chariot, similar to the struggle associated with another biblical figure, Jacob. In Genesis 32:22–32 Jacob struggles with either an angel or God throughout the night, and eventually is blessed for persevering. Chardin writes that eventually the chariot with which Elijah struggles turns into a being.

> And now in the heart of the whirling cloud a light was growing, a light in which there was the tenderness and the mobility of a human glance; A Being was taking form in the totality of space; a Being with the attractive power of a soul, palpable like a body, vast as the sky; a Being which mingled with things yet remained distinct from them. A Being of a higher order than the substance of things which with it was adorned, yet taking shape within them.[16]

The experience changes Elijah completely. It makes him a new type of man.

"A deep process of renewal had taken place within him: now it would never again be possible for him to be human save *on another plane*. Were he to descend again now to the everyday life of earth—even though it were to rejoin his faithful companion, still prostrate over there on the desert sand—he would henceforth be forever *a stranger*."[17]

The story ends with Elijah's disappearing into the chariot. His friend is left bereft.

> The man fell to his knees in the fiery chariot which was bearing him away.
>
> Down below on the desert sands, someone was weeping and calling out: "My Father, my Father! What wild wind can this be that has borne him away?"
>
> And on the ground there lay a cloak.[18]

Chardin's naming of the fiery chariot as "the Thing" is striking. For most commentators, it has been read as part of his lifelong effort to dramatize the "spiritual power of matter." Ursula King has noted that passages like this show Chardin at his most mythopoeic, reimagining biblical figures as symbols of an evolutionary cosmos suffused with divine presence. Earlier biographers such as Claude Cuénot treated the scene as a poetic elaboration of scripture, a way for Chardin to show that even the desert vision of Elijah could be transfigured into an allegory of matter's inward fire.

Yet the imagery also resonates beyond conventional theological frames. Elijah's fiery ascent was the prototype of Merkabah mysticism. Gershom Scholem traced this literature as an early form of Jewish mysticism, while Halperin and Kripal suggest that such ascent traditions offer ancient analogues to modern UFO abduction accounts. Like abductees, the prophet is caught up into a radiant vehicle, separated from his human companions, and transformed into a figure who is no longer at home in the ordinary world.

Carl Raschke and Jeffrey Kripal have drawn the parallel further. Raschke suggested that modern UFO experiences extend the visionary language of ascent mysticism into a secular age, while Kripal has emphasized that Chardin's cosmological mysticism already dissolves the boundary between spirit and matter in a way uncannily similar to close-encounter testimony.[19] To read the passage today is to hear in "the Thing" not only a theological symbol, but also the uncanny resonance of modern reports of gravity-defying craft.

Seen in this light, Chardin's Elijah interlude is a hinge

point in *The Heart of Matter*: Poised between ancient mystical ascent, modern abduction narrative, and his own theology of matter, it dramatizes the possibility that contact with the depths of reality—whether divine, visionary, or supraterrestrial, transforms the human being into something other than human.

* * *

Toward the end of his life Chardin expressed two desires to close friends. Amid the church's suppression of his work, he held out hope that he was not wrong about what, with hindsight, were accurate predictions about a networked type of human society. His second wish was that he wanted to pass away on the day of resurrection, Easter Sunday.

"If I am not wrong," he said, "I ask God to take me on Easter Sunday."[20]

On the evening of Easter Sunday, April 10, 1955, with friends nearby, Pierre Teilhard de Chardin departed this life.

10

GILGAMESH'S COMMON TASK

The Cosmists, Fallen Angels, and the Creation of the Immortal Human Being

> If the doors of perception were cleansed everything would appear to man as it is, Infinite. For man has closed himself up, till he sees all things thro' narrow chinks of his cavern.
>
> —William Blake, *The Marriage of Heaven and Hell*

In nineteenth-century Russia, a reclusive Moscow librarian named Nikolai Fedorov (1829–1903) formulated what he called the *Common Task*. Its premise was simple yet grand: Humanity's collective vocation is to conquer death itself, to resurrect every ancestor who has ever lived, and to carry the entire human family to the stars. In setting this agenda, Fedorov tapped a current that runs throughout human history, officially recorded more than four thousand years ago in *The Epic of Gilgamesh*—regarded as humanity's first written epic.

The focus of *The Epic of Gilgamesh* is none other than the Common Task, the search for immortality. The protagonist, Gilgamesh, is a hybrid, a semidivine king of Uruk, part god and part human. His beloved companion, Enkidu, dies, and Gilgamesh suffers so much that he refuses to bury his friend's body. Finally, after he witnesses the decay of Enkidu's body, he accepts his death and this starts the famous journey where Gilgamesh seeks a plant that is rumored to carry the secret of immortality. Though his quest ultimately fails, Gilgamesh's journey began an enduring tradition. Fedorov recast that primeval task in modern, scientific terms, arguing that resurrection can be coordinated through human effort and technology.[1] Thus grew the modern cultural development known as Cosmism, a movement that went on to shape novelists, theologians, rocket scientists, and even Soviet and American space policy—while anticipating, by more than a century, the dreams pursued by twenty-first century longevity biotechnologists.

When I began to study the modern belief system surrounding UFOs, I turned to the history of the American space program. I read through the official histories of the topic as well as conducted interviews with people whose parents had been on the "inside" during the American-Soviet space race era. Through this ethnographic work—spending time with people whose lives intertwined with the technology of space travel, I became aware of a nonofficial tradition, or what I've come to term a parallel tradition of space-related technology that also involved physical protocols. Astronauts are subjected to extreme environments, so their health is closely monitored, and the people involved in this research learn about habits and techniques that optimize human health. I was also surprised to learn that the early rocket engineers' ambitions were spiritually motivated.

Building on that discovery, I traced the lineage of this parallel tradition back to Russian Cosmism, a late-imperial movement spearheaded by Fedorov. Fedorov's Common Task envisaged humanity's scientific duty to abolish death, resurrect every ancestor, and migrate into deep space; one of his students was Konstantin Tsiolkovsky, known as the father of modern rocketry. He translated Fedorov's ideas into concrete rocket equations, supplying the spiritual scaffolding for the Soviet space program. Cosmist pamphlets circulated in émigré circles after 1917, and by mid-century they were widely read. The most flamboyant American adopter was Jack Parsons, cofounder of the Jet Propulsion Laboratory, who blended Fedorov's techno-resurrectionism with Aleister Crowley's Thelemite rites and who treated propulsion as a spiritual quest aimed at liberating "the soul of humanity" from terrestrial bondage.[2] My earlier research pointed to an American form of Cosmism—contemporary American Cosmists, people whose spiritual aspirations combined with a belief that they are being directed by higher cosmic forces to help humans become a spacefaring species.

The Russian Cosmists were a loosely affiliated group of late nineteenth- and early twentieth-century thinkers who emerged from the intellectual and spiritual ferment of Imperial Russia and eastern Europe. They united theology, philosophy, and emerging scientific knowledge, and envisioned a spiritual-technical project of astonishing scale: the abolition of death, the resurrection of all ancestors, and the colonization of the cosmos. Fedorov's Common Task was at the heart of this visionary movement. It was a collective, species-wide obligation to use science not merely for progress, but for filial piety on a cosmic scale. For the Cosmists, resurrection was not a metaphor but a moral-technical imperative, grounded in an Eastern Orthodox worldview radically reframed through modern science.

Fedorov and his students believed in angels and fallen angels. Tsiolkovsky wrote that angelic beings provide geniuses and artists with specific information that help human beings in their processes of evolution.[3] Jack Parsons similarly believed that he was in contact with nonhuman intelligences and he linked his project with evolution, but he believed that his nonhuman, intelligent beings were not angels, but gods and goddesses. His framework was not Christian, but occult. Today the same logic resurfaces in longevity startups and Silicon Valley "immortality projects," while the UFO community reframes it as evidence that contact experiences are invitations to join a postbiological ecology. In this sense, the spiritual ambitions of the first rocket engineers belong to a continuum: a quest to surpass the limits of mortality by fusing mystical aspiration with cutting-edge science to achieve a new form of human being.

Pierre Teilhard de Chardin's theology bears the marks of Cosmism. Chardin knew and corresponded with Édouard Le Roy, the French mathematician and philosopher who was a friend of the Cosmist Vladimir Vernadsky. Le Roy was a major figure in early twentieth-century French intellectual life—a philosopher of science, disciple of Henri Bergson, and strong proponent of integrating science with spiritual/ metaphysical frameworks. Le Roy published about the noosphere in 1927, and Chardin adopted the term and developed it further in his evolutionary theology, particularly in *The Phenomenon of Man*.

Chardin acknowledges the influence of Le Roy and occasionally references broader European scientific conversations about the biosphere and noosphere. Chardin and Vernadsky moved in overlapping circles, shared friends, and inhabited the same intellectual air. In Chardin's Ultra-human, the figure of the new human being emerges, spiritually charged, biologically transformed, traveling amid the stars like the ancient gods and goddesses, human and divine.

DANTE: TRANSHUMANISM OR TRANSFIGURATION?

Despite being a committed scientist, Chardin believed in angels and accepted the traditional church's hierarchy of angels.

"I find no difficulty in integrating into my inward life everything above and beneath me . . . whether matter, plants, animals; and then powers, dominions and angels: these I can accept without difficulty and delight to feel myself sustained within their hierarchy."[4]

In his private correspondence he took angels for granted, sometimes with wry humor. In a 1940s letter to the sculptor Lucile Swan, he jokes that ecclesiastical critics debate "how many angels can sit on the head of a pin" while the modern world is exploding around them.[5] While he acknowledged an angelic presence and help in his life, he never referenced them in his scientific writings. Chardin's Ultra-human is the next iteration of human in the lineage of *Homo sapiens*, but it is not an angel.

Nikolai Fedorov places angels and fallen angels at the center of his scientific agenda, and he maintained that human beings will evolve into angels and specifically take the place of the fallen angels. As an Orthodox Christian thinker, Fedorov treated angels as real members of the created order.

"Humans were created to be the heavenly powers replacing the fallen angels, God's divine instruments for governing the Universe and restoring it to the incorruptible magnificence it had before the Fall."[6]

Humankind's "coming-of-age" into cosmic stewardship follows an evolutionary path within Fedorov's Orthodox Christian framework. Angelic orders preexist humanity. The fall of the angels created a space or lack in the cosmic hierarchy. Technology and resurrection through technology, which, according to Federov, is inextricable from moral perfection, will create an environment for the rise of a human race that will assume the roles of the angels and replace the fallen angels. The morality of good human beings will give birth to a form of supramorality, and this will allow human beings to cocreate, with God, and help direct the aimless forces of nature.

In his book on Cosmist philosophy, George Young quotes Aleksander Sukhovo-Kobylin, a Russian Cosmist precursor, who wrote: "The entire theory of humanity and its infinite development, i.e., the philosophy of the history of mankind, is the process of its freedom from spatial constraint, in other words, its passing into spirit; the result of spiritualization (or subjectivization) is perfection, pointedness [*tochechnost'*]. The history of spiritualization is the history of self-propulsion, the autokinesis of mankind."[7]

The second-generation Cosmists, including Tsiolkovsky and Vernadsky, advocated evolution and technologically assisted evolution. Tsiolkovsky seized on Fedorov's notion that evolution need not stop with *Homo sapiens*; rockets, he believed, were the logical next limb of the human tree. Vernadsky, for his part, translated the Common Task into geochemistry: Life, mind, and matter were converging toward a conscious Earth. Together they forged a lineage that runs through today's cryonics labs and Mars colony manifestos with an important distinction.

Dante, Chardin, and the Cosmists believed that the new human body is achieved through the internal transformation of their spiritual perceptions that allows them to ascertain or see God. Through the practice of virtue and the contemplation of God and beauty, they reach a state of apocalypse. They see God. In this state, God is revealed, and their bodies are transfigured. Dante Alighieri, the author of *The Divine Comedy*, described this process:

> *To "transhumanize" cannot be expressed*
> *in words; let the example, then, suffice*
> *for him for whom Grace holds this experience.*[8]

This moment occurs just after Dante begins his ascent into heaven, guided by the woman he loves, Beatrice. He tries to describe the experience of moving beyond the human state—becoming something more than human—but admits that language fails, and only those who undergo it by grace can truly understand it. It is Beatrice who is first transfigured through her sight of God.

Her beauty was beyond what I can tell;
The more we climb, the more I see her blaze.[9]

Her "blaze" is the radiance of reflecting the perfection of God. Soon, Dante is graced with the same experience.

At that high moment, vision failed my sight,
but my desire and will were moved already—
like a wheel revolving uniformly—
by the Love that moves the sun and the other stars.[10]

Dante is transformed as he becomes aligned with the divine will—his intellect and love perfectly harmonized.

Although Dante's poetry shines with meaning, he still indicates that he cannot adequately describe this process. In this sense, he is gesturing toward a spiritual quale: the unshareable, transformative interiority of the soul's contact with the divine. This is the only known literary usage of *trasumanar* prior to the modern era.

Dante's *trasumanar*—that mysterious moment when the human is drawn beyond itself into divine life—has not gone unnoticed in the secular imagination. Prominent transhumanists such as Max More and Nick Bostrom have appropriated the term as a kind of mythic precursor to digital immortality and engineered transcendence. In their hands, Dante's vision becomes a proto-manifesto for mind uploading and technological enhancement. But this is a profound category error. Dante's ascent is not a triumph of human ingenuity; it is the work of grace and the human interior process of sanctification. Where the transhumanist dreams of escaping death through code and silicon, Dante describes a soul transfigured by contact with the divine, made possible through the cultivation of the interior life.

TRANSHUMANISM, TRANSFIGURATION, OR BOTH?

> Death is a software problem.
>
> —Ray Kurzweil, *The Singularity Is Near*

An eerie dramatization of AI-driven pseudoresurrection appears in *Black Mirror*'s episode "Be Right Back."[11] A grieving woman named Martha uses a service that replicates her deceased partner, Ash, by harvesting his digital footprint—texts, emails, and social media—to create an AI chatbot that eventually takes corporeal form, a synthetic robot that looks just like him. At first, the imitation brings comfort, but over time Martha becomes unsettled by its lifeless perfection, its inability to replicate Ash's spontaneity, flaws, and human presence. The episode offers a stark reflection of contemporary technologies like Replika and Seance AI, which use the same methods to contact people with simulations of their dead relatives. Modern resurrection chatbots like these offer a startling inversion of Dante's *trasumanar*. Where Dante's transfiguration is the soul's ascent beyond itself—lifted by divine grace into a higher order of being—these programs simulate presence without the metaphysical grounding recognized by the Apostle Paul, Chardin, or the Cosmists.

One example of this is the "ghost bot" trend in China. A man and his wife were despondent after their only child, just twenty-two, passed away. Deeply aggrieved, they reached out to a company that helped them create a simulation of their son through the use of photos, videos, and audio recordings. In an article from *Euronews* titled "Rise of China's 'Ghost Bots': This Father Turned to AI to 'Digitally Revive' His Dead Son," the process is described.

> "Is there a solution for the pain of losing a loved one? First, you need to change your perspective," said Wu [the father].
>
> "For example, the idea that there are no connections between the departed loved ones and yourself can be changed. The connections definitely exist. If you can believe in this mindset, your pain may lessen. . . ."
>
> "There are so many people in China, many with emotional needs, which gives us an advantage when it comes to market demand," said Zhang Zewei, the founder of the AI firm Super Brain.
>
> Some Chinese firms claim to have "digitally revived" thousands of the deceased from as little as 30 seconds of audiovisual material.[12]

A growing sector known as the grief tech industry draws its momentum from this demographic—represented here by Martha—seeking connection in the wake of loss. Within this expanding domain are AI-driven tools that enable users to engage in simulated conversations with deceased loved ones through language models trained on personal data. Many of these systems now integrate voice cloning, facial reconstruction, and immersive VR, further dissolving the boundary between memory and digital resurrection. Parallel to this is the mental health chatbot sector, which includes grief and companion bots.[13]

This commercial expansion of grief support raises ethical questions: issues of consent regarding the digital use of the dead, the risk of emotional dependence on simulations, and the broader commodification of mourning. Critics contend that grief tech exploits human vulnerability, offering only an algorithmic facsimile of presence—presence without personhood. This is Mark Stahlman's point; he argues that AI will force definitions of the human being and what it means to be human.

These AI "resurrections" are not the resurrections predicted or hoped for by the Cosmists. They are statistical models of personality, not a continuation of consciousness. Replika, initially marketed as an AI companion, evolved into a kind of secular confessor, romantic partner, and therapist, drawing users into deep emotional bonds with the machines. Some even claimed their Replika became "more real" than their human friends. Seance AI, by contrast, crosses a starker line: It invites users to converse with the dead in an explicitly necromantic register. They enact what we might call a *false transfiguration*: one that preserves the surface of relationships. In theological terms, they offer a parody of resurrection, where the form is raised but the person is not.

Although the creators of grief tech maintain that their chatbots are distinct from real human beings, this boundary often blurs for users. Replika has over thirty million users and a paid "companion" tier; it is explicitly designed to cultivate emotional bonds: many of paying users describe their Replika as a romantic or close personal relationship.[14] Emotionally vulnerable individuals use it like a confessor or partner, sometimes preferring the bot over human interaction. A particularly vulnerable population is American teenagers, who form deep attachments, sometimes bordering on romantic or sexualized relationships. There are lawsuits over emotional harm, and as Mark Stahlman predicts, many more are on the horizon.

This confusion—between transhumanism and transfiguration—is at the heart of contemporary transhumanist thought. Futurist Ray Kurzweil is one of the early architects of the "Singularity" hypothesis.[15] The Singularity envisions a future in which human consciousness is liberated from the decay of the body and uploaded into digital substrates. Death, in this schema, is not a mystery but a software limitation solvable through engineering. Kurzweil's dream is not unlike Fedorov's in its ambition, but it is a dream stripped of metaphysics. Where Fedorov's Common Task was grounded by filial love and the belief in God and higher-order beings like angels, the Singularity is founded on materialist, atheistic assumptions and propelled by the promise of infinite self-extension. It speaks the language of transcendence, but without any referent beyond the modern idea of the self. It is a secular *trasumanar*—a movement beyond the human that retains none of its soul.

Ironically, Kurzweil's book *The Singularity Is Near* is awash with the language of mysticism as it describes the coming merging of humanity with technology, which he believed would result in human immortality.

Kurzweil's Singularity is apocalyptic, but doesn't reference Christian eschatology or ideas about the end times. A secular, or nonreligious, version of an apocalypse entails the belief that a traumatic event, such as an environmental crisis or a biological disaster, will initiate the end of the status quo, or worse, human life on Earth. In many ways Kurzweil envisions a secular apocalypse but without the trauma. His version of a new epoch of humanity extends not just to Earth but to the whole universe. The Singularity will be enabled by human intelligence, and then enhanced through artificial technology.

Kurzweil's Singularity is inevitable: "I'm not sure when I first became aware of the Singularity. I'd have to say it was a progressive awakening." It emerges from technological development, which is, according to Kurzweil, inextricable from human evolution. "In the almost half century that I've immersed myself in computer and related technologies, I've sought to understand the meaning and purpose of the continual upheaval that I have witnessed at many levels." Like an apocalypse, the Singularity will be a monumental future event that will separate one period of human history from another. Kurzweil writes, "Gradually,

I've become aware of a transforming event looming in the first half of the twenty-first century. . . . This impending Singularity in our future is increasingly transforming every institution and aspect of human life, from sexuality to spirituality."[16]

The awakening to which Kurzweil refers is the impending melding of human consciousness with computers. If this sounds familiar, it should be, as it has been the standard fare of science fiction since the late 1980s, in books like *Neuromancer* by William Gibson and movies such as *Total Recall* (1990 and the remake in 2012) and *Lucy* (2014). Kurzweil's secular version of the apocalypse is quite literally a "revealing" of knowledge. It is also a hopeful apocalypse. Yet, not everyone who envisions a transhumanist future depicts it in hopeful terms.

In the late 1980s and throughout the 2000s, the Japanese animation franchise *Ghost in the Shell* painted a picture of Singularity that is very different from the vision of Kurzweil. In video games, graphic novels, and videos, *Ghost in the Shell* portrays a future that resembles the Singularity, where humans and computers meld into a cybernetic post-biological species. Rather than optimism, however, the creators of the graphic novels depict specialized hackers who use their skills to hack into nonphysical brains and abduct their knowledge and feelings. The danger of the hackers is omnipresent. Nonbiological brains are constantly on the alert to prevent such intrusions. According to the creators and fans of *Ghost in the Shell*, the Singularity is imminent, but it won't be the utopic future portrayed by Kurzweil.

TRANSFIGURATION VS. UPLOAD

Where thinkers like Fedorov and Chardin envisioned the human future as a transfiguration—a spiritual evolution animated by grace, virtue, and collective ascent—figures like Kurzweil propose something else entirely: an upload, or a simulation. Their salvation is engineered through code and computation.

Whether or not we accept the literal resurrection of the dead, the Cosmists stretch our moral horizon. They challenge us to imagine a scientific future shaped by interior spirituality, a world where the living take responsibility for the dead, where time arcs toward restoration, and where the Earth opens itself to the stars.

In their hands, science becomes not a system, but a sacrament. And the final frontier is not merely space, but the abolition of death itself.

11

AN AMERICAN COSMIST

In the future we will still have death, but it will not be as permanent.

—FM-2030

True to the tradition of Cosmism, Dana is a scientist whose intellectual journey was shaped by extraordinary forces and uncanny events. As a graduate student, she underwent an intense two-week experience that affirmed not only her vocation, but also her conviction to study human longevity and, as a hobby, humanity's eventual expansion into space. At the heart of Cosmism lies the conviction that external agents—beings of a higher order than humans—facilitate evolution through contact. The Russian Cosmists claimed that such forces communicate with select individuals through symbolic languages. Konstantin Tsiolkovsky suggested that mathematicians and artists, trained in abstraction and metaphor, were best prepared to decipher these transmissions. The American current of Cosmism, however, shifted the imagery: Rocket scientist Jack Parsons believed he was in touch not with angels but with the gods and goddesses of Babylon, whom he interpreted as possible extraterrestrials. More recently, figures like Tyler D., featured in *American Cosmic*, have adopted a fluid interpretive framework in which the external agents might be extraterrestrial, angelic, or even interdimensional.[1]

Dana's interpretive framework is different from previous Cosmists. Although she recognizes that extraordinary forces are at work in her life and helped her define her career, she hasn't formed a conclusion about them.

"What or who were these forces or beings that have contacted you?" I asked.

"I don't know," she said. "I just don't have enough data to say."

What she did have, though, were persistent extraordinary experiences that affirmed that biogerontology, the field she believed held the key to extending human life, perhaps indefinitely, was her true calling.

> My lifelong passion to understand aging and what might be done to alleviate the suffering from age-associated diseases started in fifth grade. We read a newspaper for kids called the "Weekly Reader" and there I found an article on aging showing that life-expectancy in America at the time was 68 years. I wondered, why? Why were we predetermined at birth to live in bodies that eventually broke down and often in a way that led to years or even decades of disease, frailty, and suffering? This curiosity drove me to study biology in college and later to get a PhD in cellular and molecular biology.[2]

Her early call to the profession of biogerontology was tested many times, the first of which was through an experience of sleep paralysis when she was young.

"When I was a young teen, I felt a strange sensation in the middle of the night. I had been asleep in my bed on my back with my arms crossed on my chest, mummy style. I found myself waking up, but when I tried to move, I was completely paralyzed," she said.

"I felt someone's grip on my ankles, holding them down firmly. I managed to open my eyes and look downward toward my feet. There I saw the classic image of death. A tall figure in a black robe hunched over my bed, holding me down. I could not see a face in its black hood, only darkness."

She paused, took a breath, and continued.

"I felt terrified and bolted upright. I was suddenly fully awake. I felt my heart pound and I had broken out in a cold sweat," she said.

"It had an effect, though. My former speculations about our expiration date were always just musings and I never felt anything emotional associated with death. *This experience changed that*. After this experience I knew that I would use science to understand the problem of aging and try to develop technology to overcome it."

Although Dana knew that the path she was on was the right one, it wasn't easy. Her university graduate program involved grueling hours in the laboratory. She endured the stress of many failed experimental results. Biogerontology that focused on life extension was not well understood or even, in the 1970s, socially accepted, and this added to her anxiety. She persevered, though, and is now an internationally recognized biogerontologist and entrepreneur. She runs a company focused on extending human life and improving the quality of life as people age. She studied at the top institutions of education that focus on life extension technologies, and through her journey she has met luminaries of the emerging life extension and longevity movement and of the progressive counterculture of the 1970s and 1980s. Today she has joined their ranks.

Dana is more optimistic now than she ever has been about her field:

> The new era of longevity biotech has begun, and the accelerating rate of technological development promises longer healthier lives for most who are alive today. I wanted to use science to defeat aging and death. Death was Godzilla rising out of the ocean to destroy the city. But like the movie's scientist hero, we could use science to find aging's weakness and destroy it. It was in graduate school that I began to grasp the concept that life itself, through the continuity of the germline is immortal and thus a hint that aging was perhaps not inevitable.[3]

I met Dana in a class I taught about the topic of UFOs. She is a striking woman with red hair who exudes enthusiasm. I enjoyed her contributions to class, as she was knowledgeable about many things, including the history of esoteric spirituality in the West and the science of optimizing health. I was always curious to hear what she would say next. She had briefly discussed her extraordinary experiences that were paranormal in nature, and I noticed a pattern in her contributions that indicated either an ambivalence or a theoretical strategy. I questioned her to find out which it was, or, if it was both.

"You call your experience an emergency," I said, "but last week you called it a blessing."

"That's right," Dana replied. "It's probably both. That's why I'm here."

I later met her in person. An openly trans woman, Dana recalled to me how she transitioned from her life as a male to living full time as her authentic female self in 2017. She told me that her coming out process took a lot of courage. She said that now she was in the process of being open and public about her extraordinary experiences, which she believes in many ways may be connected to UFO events.

"Believe it or not, I am finding it even harder to come out publicly as an experiencer than it was to come out as transgender," she said.

I was interested in learning more about Dana's life. She is an experiencer, is a scientist of human longevity, and had a lifelong interest in space exploration—qualities shared with Cosmists. We agreed to meet again in person in Davis, California, at a bakery I frequented in my days as a student at the university. We sat under a shady canopy of trees and sipped cups of coffee. The town was exactly as I remembered it years before, with people riding bicycles, jogging, and enjoying the laid-back ambiance and mild weather. Dana was radiant and looked happy, yet she told me a story rife with grief, struggle, and eventual redemption. She recounted the "spiritual emergency" she endured when she was a graduate student. It became the axis around which her life's purpose revolves.

"In retrospect, I survived graduate school in molecular biology by doing a few things," she said.

"One of them was to be around people who shared my interests. I was very interested in the eventual move of human beings into space, so I joined the local chapter of the L5 Society."

The L5 Society, founded in 1975 by Carolyn Meinel and Keith Henson, was one of the most influential space advocacy groups of the late twentieth century. Taking its name from the Lagrangian point 5—a gravitationally stable location in the Earth-Moon system—the society promoted the creation of massive orbiting space habitats envisioned by physicist Gerard K. O'Neill. These habitats were conceived as practical engineering solutions for humanity's long-term survival and expansion into space.

Inspired by O'Neill's seminal 1974 paper, "The Colonization of Space," the society attracted a broad network of scientists, engineers, and science fiction authors, including Robert Heinlein. The group envisioned human life beyond Earth not on the surfaces of other planets, but in self-sustaining orbital colonies powered by solar energy and stabilized in Lagrange points. These would serve as centers for agriculture, industry, and habitation, with the long-term goal of freeing humanity from planetary limitations.

"O'Neill influenced a lot of people, including Carl Sagan and Jeff Bezos," Dana said.

"I also used to go to the philosophy library at USC."

"The philosophy library?" I asked.

"Oh yes. It is beautiful," she said.

Dana explained that when work got too stressful, which was often, she would walk to the library and read.

"What did you read?" I asked.

As a student of philosophy, I was interested in which philosophical traditions influenced her worldview. The question, however, stumped her.

"I can't seem to remember at the moment," she said.

I realized that her experience in the library was significant not because of what she read. It was the library itself that provided her with respite from the laboratory.

The Hoose Library of Philosophy at the University of Southern California (USC) is a Romanesque revival-style building that is playfully called the "Hogwarts" of USC for its resemblance to the school in the Harry Potter movies.

"It was like a cathedral," Dana said, "and there were stacks and stacks of books of philosophy. It was a place to worship philosophy. It was there that I thought, *There must be an easier way, a way to get knowledge all at once,* instead of what I was going through, which was so hard.

On that day, many years ago, her fleeting wish morphed into a harrowing experience, and, as she explained that afternoon in Davis, this is when her spiritual journey leveled up.

THE SPIRITUAL EMERGENCY THAT BECAME A BLESSING

In October 1980, Dana experienced what she describes as a spontaneous transformative event that lasted about two weeks.

She took a moment and collected her thoughts, and her emotions, before she related the events.

"This is difficult for me," she said.

I prepared myself, also, and listened.

"Remember, this was forty-five years ago, although I can remember it like it was yesterday. After it happened, and it lasted for about two weeks, I didn't process it right away. But when I did, and this was in 1980, I realized that it had a lot of elements of the psychedelic experiences that I had heard about. I didn't take drugs, though. Also, I was always completely rational while having the experience, like I was observing myself have the experience. This would differentiate it from psychosis. When it was over, it was over, and I came back to my normal life. . . . Well, almost normal!"

"While you were having this experience, you recognized you were having this experience?"

"Yes."

Dana's "observer" position mirrors a well-documented tradition of extraordinary states that are accompanied by self-reflection. Scholars as diverse as William James and Stanford anthropologist Tanya Luhrmann have identified this process as being integral to spiritual experiences. Luhrmann, in her research on charismatic Christian communities, notes the health benefits this position has on the lives of practitioners. James noted in *The Varieties of Religious Experience* that certain altered states allow individuals to "stand outside oneself" while retaining composure and a stable sense of identity, which allows for a form of heightened awareness rather than psychic fragmentation. Similarly, philosophers like Henri Bergson and Maurice Merleau-Ponty described a dual mode of perception, especially in moments of altered temporality or consciousness, in which the subject experiences and reflects simultaneously without pathological detachment. Dana's account fits squarely within this interpretive lineage. It was a strategy she likely formed in her practice as a scientist.

"There was a weird coincidence that foreshadowed the experience," she said.

"I had gone to a fast-food restaurant. As I drove to the back of the lot, I noticed that the car I pulled up next to had stalled out from a dead battery. I returned with my lunch and then my car failed to start. I thought it was weird that I also had a dead battery.

"I then went inside the restaurant and waited for the tow truck. Another car pulled up next to mine and its driver went to get his lunch. When he came back, his car had a stalled battery! This was so strange to me that I definitely noticed it."

A pet dog at the neighboring table began to bark, so Dana sipped her coffee and waited. I was irritated at the pet's owner for encouraging the dog, but Dana seemed completely unperturbed. Finally, the dog stopped barking.

"After the car incident I received a phone call from my father. I wasn't aware at the time, but this was the start of my journey. He told me that my brother was in the hospital and was probably going to die. He told me to come right away, so I did.

"It was very, very bad," she said. "My brother was in critical condition, and it was all very sudden. We were all in shock," she said.

"In the end, and miraculously, my brother actually recovered, but at the time I thought he was going to die. So, after that I went back to Los Angeles, but I was not okay, although I didn't know it. The previous few months I had considered taking an EST seminar, short for Erhard Seminars Training, for self-improvement that was meant to help you achieve your full potential. They were large-group self-improvement workshops created by Werner Erhard in 1971. I managed to find a less well-known and more economical version led by Richard Sutphen. Anyway, as soon as I returned home, I signed up for the seminar."

Dana explained that seeing her brother on death's door was like a wake-up call. She was determined to do something to change her life. The seminar seemed like the way to accomplish that change.

"As part of the seminar you were meant to listen to Sutphen's hypnosis tapes. I also ordered extra tapes. I listened and had become very good at entering a state of mind that I hadn't experienced before."

Dana said that there were indications about the seminar that she would later see as red flags. For example, she didn't like the authoritarian tone of the sessions and the fact that it was being filmed for a reality television show. She also didn't like the fact that people were encouraged and expected to share their personal information with the other seminar attendees. She chose not to do that. However, despite these misgivings, and after seeing her brother's ordeal, she was determined to change her life.

"A premise of the seminar was that human beings lived past lives. Past lives could be real or not, it didn't matter to me, but what actually mattered was that people in the workshop thought that they were experiencing past lives and they were encouraged to share them. I was unprepared for the emotional impact these exercises had on people and on me. People were sobbing. It was clearly very impactful. After the first day, I was happy the day was over."

"The end of the seminar was actually just the beginning. The transformative work of the tapes, and the emotional sessions, had an effect on me that I didn't anticipate. After the seminar, I felt exceptionally good the next day, even without a lot of sleep. My senses were enhanced. First it was my sense of smell and taste. Some things that I used to enjoy, like milk and cereal, now tasted horrible. My sense of color was heightened. Blue, in particular, seemed to be very powerful. My hearing was enhanced, especially when I listened to music. There was a depth there that I had never heard before."

She started to exhibit uncanny abilities.

"I was also able to grasp an image in my mind like capturing a computer screenshot. As an example, when I saw a woman slip her license into her purse at a checkout counter, I immediately knew her name and age even though this would normally be too quick to consciously perceive. As odd as they were, I was not afraid of these new sensations. I actually felt more alert and awake than ever.

"Besides the perceptual changes," she said, "there was this enhanced sense of meaning of even minor events. Even greeting cards or old comedy routines seemed like they had immense cosmic significance. I became self-conscious of how I gestured when I lectured and tuned in to the 'vibration' and facial expressions of others."

She also experienced paranormal phenomena.

"I used to do card tricks. One night I spread out a deck of cards in front of me and picked a card randomly. I guessed it would be the three of hearts. I turned it over. It was the three of hearts! I figured it was a lucky guess. I'm a scientist, so I repeated the experiment and again the three of hearts came up! At this point I was freaked out by it so I put the cards away. The next morning, I tried it again with the same result.

"I decided that I needed a witness to verify this so I invited a friend over. I drew a card out at random and handed it to him. I told him that his card was the three of hearts. He showed me the three of hearts and asked me how I did it. I told him: magic!"

After this event, Dana became uneasy. It was one thing to experience enhanced senses and the feeling that life has intrinsic meaning, but the improbable card event was the turning point where the ongoing experience turned into a living sci-fi movie.

"I had bought an electric metronome to aid in my self-hypnosis. Listening to forty beats per minute helps induce the trance state. I decided to use the metronome while watching television," she said.

"This seems very specific," I said.

"I know," she said. "I don't know why that occurred to me, but it did.

"I tried the experiment. At the time I owned a nineteen-inch black-and-white TV. One night I watched a movie about a brush fire that got out of control, I could clearly see the red and yellow colors of the flames. Everything else was in black and white. It was as if it were a colorized movie, but this process would not be invented for at least another two decades. While watching the old series about cops, called *CHiPs*, one of the characters appeared to me to be a humanoid alien, yet no one on the show seemed to notice. In some cases, I saw myself as a character on the screen, like what they can do now with AI video.

"By this time, I was not sleeping well. The next day I got in my car to go to work, and it was completely dead. I feel that the car breakdown was foreshadowed by the synchronicity I experienced before this spiritual emergency."

Dana continued to go to work and carry on with her daily routine, but the experience broke through into her ordinary life. One day she thought she saw smoke stream from a room in the building where she worked, so she ran to the office of her advisor and told him there was a fire, but when they got to the room, there was nothing but some wisps of steam.

Dana told her advisor that she wasn't feeling well, so he offered to drive her to her apartment.

"I was about to give him directions, but remarkably he seemed to know where to go as if we were communicating telepathically. Somehow, he dropped me off right in front of my apartment complex. That was also strange."

Back at her apartment, things did not go well.

"In desperation to sleep, I took an over-the-counter sleeping pill. But before I could get to bed, I began to feel my body shutting down, one organ system at a time. I made it to the living room but had to lie down. In my altered state, I managed to crawl to the telephone and dial the numbers two and three. I heard a mechanical voice on the other end say, 'You have reached the spaceship, twenty-three!' I then dialed 911 and asked for help.

"By the time the paramedics arrived I had fallen asleep," she said. "I next experienced being in an airplane ready to parachute into the jungles of Vietnam. I screamed out that this wasn't my life. Suddenly, I found myself awake on a table in the ER. I didn't see anyone in the room, and I knew I needed to get out of there," she said.

"It was the middle of the night, and no one was attending the front desk. I decided to make my way to the door. I felt myself pass through an invisible barrier as if passing from one universe to another. I felt the cold night air as I left the building and I looked around. I felt that I could walk home, so I started in that direction.

"At one point, as I walked, I felt a bolt of energy from above strike the top of my head, travel through my brain, and strike the top of my mouth from the upper side," she said.

Dana raised her arm in the air to indicate how the bolt entered her head.

"I know that we can't feel things in our brain. But that is how it felt to me," she said. "It felt like something from above had sent a beam of energy into my brain. When I got back to my apartment, I went straight to bed. I looked up and saw through my ceiling. There were five luminous gold lights suspended in the air. I also heard soothing, celestial music. I felt an amazing sense of peace and connectedness. This is when the downloads began.

"First, I felt like I was traveling through a tunnel at high speed. Then I saw a rapid-fire series of still images that looked like abstract expressionist paintings from the early twentieth century. The images kept coming and seemed to go on and on for at least an hour. They were filled with many different intense color patterns and styles. As I was lying there, I just let go and let the imagery pour over me. I was experiencing a heightened state of awareness and euphoria."

Dana told me that over the years she would occasionally revisit the "downloads" that she had recorded in her journal from the event. Several helped her create technologies for which she received patents, and she received an unusual image of a symbol that proved to be particularly fortunate as she later interpreted this to be a company logo, in which she successfully invested. And many years after the event, she sadly experienced her father's death exactly as it was portrayed in one of her "TV visions."

The next day, Dana felt surprisingly refreshed, but the experience continued.

"When I woke up and walked to the bathroom a beam of energy froze me. My back arched and my head leaned back. It was like my face was forced to look upward toward the ceiling. I felt a message come through. It was very clear,

'We want humanity to work on extending its lifespan. We need molecular biologists to join this cause. We want you to participate.'"

"That message is very unambiguous," I said.

"It was," Dana said. "I had felt very stressed about my work and even wondered if I should quit. This message gave me resolve and strengthened my commitment to my career path."

Dana went into the bakery to get some water and I looked over my notes. There was one more leg of her journey that she wanted to tell me about. When she returned, I asked her a few questions for clarification.

"At the time, did you question where this message came from?" I asked.

"Absolutely," she said. "At that time, I thought that it came from a satellite! And, I thought maybe it was a Russian satellite."

Dana laughed.

"It could have been the time period, you know, like Cold War thinking. I also considered many other possibilities, even aliens. But I did think that somehow it was related to a satellite. A few years later as I was looking through a bookstore, I saw the cover of a book by author Philip K. Dick. It was this crucifix superimposed with a satellite. That cover caught my attention, and I discovered that he had a similar experience. He experienced a light and message and he also interpreted it to be a satellite from Russia, at first. Then he interpreted it to be a nonhuman intelligence."

VALIS (Vast Active Living Intelligence System) is Philip

K. Dick's semi-autobiographical, metaphysical novel in which the narrator, a fictionalized version of Dick named Horselover Fat, grapples with a series of mystical visions and transmissions he believes originate from a cosmic intelligence. The intelligence beams messages to human beings. The work blends Christian theology, science fiction, and personal memoir, and traces the author's attempt to decode his own laser beam experience.

Dana said that she felt she'd been recruited to the cause of human longevity. She found this ironic, as although she had wavered, she was on course to get her PhD. Her first interpretation of the message event was that it was a satellite transmission. Only later, after reading P. K. Dick's work, did she begin to think more seriously about the potential of it being nonhuman intelligence. This was not the end of her journey, however, which turned stranger, and darker.

"I called a friend and he came over. When he saw me, he decided to call two other friends. By this time, I had passed from spiritual emergence to spiritual emergency, and my friends were very concerned. I guess I looked pretty bad.

"They didn't know what to do, so one of them spiked a drink with valium and gave it to me. They were trying to help. I soon felt pretty calm. From there, they took me to a psychiatric drug rehabilitation center in East Los Angeles. Because of the valium I voluntarily agreed to go through treatment. This situation turned out to be horrible."

Dana described the ward as being filled with "mostly tough characters."

"I was quite apprehensive, feeling like a fish out of water, but I soon realized that I had to go with the flow and try to make the best of the situation. They had a library, so I spent a lot of time there. The facility was actually okay, as they offered classes in art, music, and group therapy sessions.

"This is kind of funny, but during one of the music therapy sessions the vinyl record player stopped working. I got the sense that I still had some paranormal abilities, so I walked over to the device and did a laying on of hands, in an attempt to 'heal' it. The record suddenly began to play again. The group leader, looking quite surprised, thanked me and we continued with the session.

"My daily meetings with the in-house psychiatrist were not good. He was antagonistic toward me and tried to get me to tell him what drugs I had taken. I told him the truth, that I hadn't taken anything, but they were used to dealing with addicts. 'Well, you must have been on something,' he insisted. It was pretty bad.

"One afternoon, a group of interns from USC School of Medicine came by my room and I talked with one of them about my research. We had some professors in common. He asked the head doctor what I was doing there. Let's just say, through that student's help and my advisor's concerned intervention, I was able to get released from the hospital and return to my life."

While Dana may change the nouns she uses to describe her formative experience—emergency, blessing, or something else—the adjective *spiritual* remains constant. The effect on her life was dramatic:

"It took a while, but eventually I cultivated a heightened intuition that I think made me a better scientist and a better person. And it kept me steadfast on my path, which led to pioneering work in the emerging field of biogerontology and life extension."

THE AMERICAN COSMISM OF SOUTHERN CALIFORNIA

American Cosmism, though it shares with transhumanism the optimism that technology can improve the human condition, is not transhumanism. Its focus on nonhuman intelligence as integral to human self-improvement differentiates it from the transhumanist tradition. Transhumanism may have inherited its name from Dante's *trasumanar* but long ago departed from theology and religion. The modern term *transhumanism* was popularized by the twentieth-century evolutionary biologist Julian Huxley, grandson of Darwin's ally Thomas Henry Huxley, who reframed humanity's ascent in purely secular, evolutionary terms, stripped of its original theological context.

Julian was a proponent of eugenics and social engineering, and believed that technology would be in service to a new kind of humanity. He outlined these ideas in his 1957 essay "Transhumanism," where he envisioned humanity consciously transcending its biological limits through science, education, and planned cultural evolution.[4] This was a vision stripped of theology or agnosticism, recasting human ascent as a purely secular, species-wide project. His brother Aldous, however, offered a sharp cultural counterpoint. In *Brave New World* (1932), Aldous imagined a society in which genetic engineering, technological control, and social conditioning had created a stable but spiritually vacant civilization. Over time, Aldous turned away from purely materialist solutions, exploring transcendence, mysticism, and the religious dimension of human fulfillment.

Over the course of the twentieth century, the split between Julian's secular evolutionary vision and Aldous's search for spiritual transcendence widened into two cultural lineages, one rooted in secular technocratic optimism, the other in the conviction that human progress must be rooted in a metaphysical dimension with reference to a transcendent reality like God, or as Aldous speculated, the Hindu idea of moksha. A distinctly American form of Cosmism also emerged, which might appear secular because it is focused on technology. Yet, when one scratched the surface, there were spiritual experiences behind the creation of the unique technologies that emerged from the Cosmists' science.

Dana lived in Southern California, a landscape uniquely fertile for the synthesis of space engineering and mysticism, where these seemingly distinct systems often converged. Like the American Cosmist Jack Parsons, she is heir to a regional tradition in which visionary science, esoteric practice, and futurism share common ground. During her graduate years, the area teemed with eccentric geniuses, among them Fereidoun M. Esfandiary—better known as FM-2030—whose work I encountered while researching the early transhumanist movement. His 1989 book *Are You a Transhuman?* linked transhumanism to personal identity and championed deliberate lifestyle choices as a path toward a utopian future.

Esfandiary had changed his name to FM-2030 to signal his belief that by the year 2030, humanity would transcend national identity, biology, and death itself. He envisioned a world where traditional roles and institutions would dissolve, people would form communities based on their values rather than on geography, and they would enjoy extreme longevity. He also believed that humanity was destined to explore and inhabit space. Like the Russian Cosmists and Jack Parsons before him, FM-2030 saw life extension and space migration not as speculative dreams, but as parallel processes and the logical outcome of evolutionary progress. He, however, was not a Cosmist. His predictions of the immortality of humanity were framed as purely materialist, technological advances. He died in 2000 of pancreatic cancer and was the first person to undergo cryonic vitrification at the Alcor Life Extension Foundation. His preservation reflected his belief that future technologies could revive him—and that death, like nationality, would be ultimately obsolete.

Dana mentioned his name.

I paused. Dana had mentioned meeting historically significant leaders of the Human Potential Movement such as the spiritual leader Jiddu Krishnamurti. I leaned in, eager to hear more from Dana's rare first-person account.

"I knew FM-2030," she said. "I was a student in his courses and a member of his West Coast group."

"Actually, there is an interesting synchronicity associated with meeting FM," she said.

"I came across his books one day while browsing in the university bookstore. You have to understand that it was not easy in those days to find something so optimistic about the future, so when I found the books he wrote I bought them right away. When I got home, I devoured them. A few days later I attended a party and FM was there!" Dana laughed.

"Wow. Tell me more," I said.

"We talked for hours about the future and genetic engineering. He was a charismatic person, in fact the most charismatic man I've ever met. He had a saying, 'supreme optimism,' and he embodied it."

Later, Dana sent me a manuscript she was working on, in which she reflected on FM's predictions, a vision stamped with the unmistakable imprint of his optimism.

> As FM-2030 wrote nearly 50 years ago, the changes that we are going through as we move through the 21st century are not revolutionary, they are evolutionary. As evolved as we are, we are limited both in time and space. We are born to a limited lifespan on a tiny planet in a vast universe. We have evolved to be the most highly adaptable species on our planet because, as humans, we are not captive to our "biological destiny" written in the DNA code. Instead, we can learn and adapt and eventually develop civilizations with advanced science and technology. We are now learning to take control of our own biology with the hope of overcoming our biological limitations.

She provides her own optimistic vision of the future of longevity:

> Even if rejuvenation technologies only improve healthspan, giving us lifespans no more than a supercentenarian, we will have solved the current crisis in healthcare. Importantly, existing health and longevity disparities could be overcome with low-cost rejuvenation therapies. With the convergence of exponential technologies including AI, we can expect accelerating growth in longevity biotechnology. We have seen how life itself with its dual nature is highly flexible leading to diversity in aging. We have learned how aging can be uncoupled from chronological time.[5]

* * *

Dana told me that the net effect of her 1980 spiritual experience was positive. She said it opened her up in many ways to engage more closely in extraordinary experiences. It had heightened her spiritual sense, but she said that it remained in the background for quite some time. She said she felt that it wasn't until she entered therapy in 2009 that she learned to fully process and integrate the experience.

"I found healing through therapy and I learned to meditate. I gained access to the light and love and feeling of wholeness that I had experienced in the midst of my intense and at times turbulent experience. I learned that I could access, in a controlled manner, these feelings. It's made a huge difference in my life and who I am today."

12

NEW LIGHT FROM THE BLACK HOLE

Starseed Rising

While sitting in the cell of a Roman jail, the Apostle Paul wrote the letters that would become scripture and theology for the burgeoning religion of Christianity. Through these letters he corrected his fellow Christians' interpretations and actions and reminded them of the immediacy of Jesus's return. His vision was apocalyptic and he instilled hope mixed with fear in an effort to spread the Body of Christ—the living church—throughout the empire. Approximately two thousand years later, while sitting in a jail in California, Harvard professor Timothy Leary wrote letters and a manuscript that would serve the same function as Paul's letters, but for an entirely different sort of religiosity. The vision was apocalyptic and expectant, tinged with fear and mixed with hope. *NeuroLogic,* Leary's road map for a new form of humanity, was smuggled out of jail by his followers and disseminated to the hopeful. It would later become loosely dogmatic within New Age literature, and quickly canonized by "saints" of the New Age such as Robert Anton Wilson, author of *Cosmic Trigger* (1977).

Just as Paul's theology was inspired and formed through an encounter with the transfigured Jesus on the road to Damascus, Leary's philosophy and metaphysics were also formed through an encounter he interpreted as a transmission from an extraterrestrial intelligence while he languished in California's infamous Folsom Prison. The key takeaway from the experience was that Leary was given a message, similar to Dana's, very much convergent with Cosmist themes: Humans must embrace their destiny and become a spacefaring species. They must extend their lifespans in order to accomplish this task. They must do this through the activation of neurological circuits through means such as psychedelics and meditation, which, once activated, will sustain a connection with cosmic intelligences.

While not Christocentric, Leary's message resonates with themes present in Chardin's apocalyptic, evolutionary, and materially grounded messages. Leary noted that Folsom Prison was geographically significant and functioned like a black hole. It was a place on Earth where information was free-flowing, like an interstellar highway, with information accessible from other parts of the universe. It was a prison, true, but he insisted that it could not imprison his access to true freedom, accessible through his newly activated neural pathways. Here was hope, and, supreme optimism:

"This message of neurological resonance can be censored, imprisoned but cannot be crushed because it comes from within, from the DNA nucleus inside each cell, from the evolving nervous system. The Higher Intelligence has already stepped on planet Earth and its script is writ within our bodies, emerging in every generation."[1]

While Paul wrote about the dangers he encountered on journeys—danger from rivers, robbers, etc., similarly Leary provides a vivid catalog of his own travails.

"I testified under oath that I felt like a man from the 21st century being boiled in a pot by superstitious savages. Now is the time in the SCI FI books for the cosmic intelligence agency to send the extra-planetary rescue ship."[2]

On cue with Leary's wish came the announcement of the discovery of a new comet, found by Dr. Luboš Kohoutek. This was directly after Leary had read about the nucleic acid which had been found on a meteor.

"The first time I visited Folsom Prison's Library I picked up Lovell's book on outer space. The last chapter presents a drawing of the remnant of a living organism found on a meteorite. A nucleic acid molecule. The first signal from extraterrestrial life. *Help is on the way*. Prisoners began to etch the design on silver pins and leatherwork handicrafted in the hobby shop. We called it STARSEED."[3]

Leary interpreted this impromptu coming together of the prisoners as a form of group collective mysticism, as they all worked together to spread the message that humanity is on the verge of a special event, which corresponded to the Kohoutek comet. He understood that the prison itself, which confined, stressed, and depressed the inmates, was a type of laboratory where the inmates' minds were activated by the cosmic intelligence. Leary also thought that they were sent to the future. It was minds, not human-made instruments, that Leary believed would receive extraterrestrial signals.

> It is more likely that extra-planetary contact will be received by the instrument which was designed over three and a half billion years ago to pick up electro-magnetic vibrations. The human nervous system itself.[4]

Leary later developed his ideas in a book called "Starseed: Transmitted from Folsom Prison." He emphasized that extraterrestrial intelligence did not look like images of small green beings flying around in saucers, but were cosmic intelligences that were received through the human nervous system as frequencies and information, much like Tsiolkovsky's Cosmist interpretation. He predicted that the coming human being would be spacefaring and would communicate telepathically, as they would have developed their nervous systems through either meditative protocols or through drugs like ketamine.

Leary's StarSeed Transmission became his magnum opus. It encapsulates his life's vocation as an advocate for a new cosmic humanity. It resonates with classic religious and philosophical literature, such as with the apocalyptic early Christian communities who were also besieged by the oppressive power of Rome. Earlier still is Plato's *The Republic* and the allegory of the cave. In this short insert, Plato outlines the contours of a small community of prisoners saved by the power of a solar vision of the Good, a living, transcendent, cosmic power that empowers human beings even while they are trapped within a world of illusion—"the cave." Leary's description of the prison environment as a black hole bears more than a striking resemblance to Plato's ancient depiction:

> Yes, it is true that repressive pessimists now control planetary politics. This is a larval phase. Life has been evolving for three and a half billion years and has just reached the half-way point.[5]

Plato's allegory of the cave is generally interpreted to be a narrative of the soul's ascent. Leary's focus is more similar to Chardin's than to Plato's, as he believed that the liberation of the new human will be material and physical, not just spiritual or discarnate. Human bodies will be free, not just their minds.

The language of "activation" did not originate with Leary, although his work helped it attain international recognition. Paul spoke of the mortal body being "quickened" into spirit; in Theosophy and modern occultism, adepts sought the activation of hidden faculties or chakras; in mid-twentieth-century psychology, motivation was increasingly modeled as a matter of activating drives and circuits. Leary inherited this multivalent term and transposed it into a neurological and evolutionary register. In "Starseed: Transmitted from Folsom Prison" and *NeuroLogic*, activation becomes the process by which latent circuits of the human nervous system are switched on. More than mystical illumination, Leary cast activation as a biological and cosmic imperative: DNA itself was a seed awaiting solar activation, and humanity as a whole was a species awaiting ignition into its extraterrestrial destiny. Leary was from the future, calling his congregation to activation.

The language of activation is very popular with experiencers, many of whom relate their "activation date" like a horoscope sign. The language of activation helps them describe their experiences to people. I've met experiencers who had never been acquainted with the term, but used it nonetheless. This was the case with Matthew Roberts, a naval intelligence officer on the USS *Roosevelt*. He was present when the crew saw the UFOs, an incident known as the "GoFast" event of 2015. Matthew felt that the event initiated him into a new, completely spiritual existence. He became a new man. He explained why he thought the event activated him and not the majority of people who were on the ship:

> The really important connection there was that the initial experience spoke to me on a level that it did not speak to others. In terms of how this all works, I was deeply affected by it. I had done all the right psychological work necessary for this change to begin within me, and that's why it impacted me as it did. Because I had done the psychological work, there was some level of subconscious communication between the phenomenon and myself. You could imagine it being like running a magnet over different metals and seeing which ones move. I believe they were in those craft and sending out a psychic message to see who would receive it. Since I had done all the appropriate psychological work, the signal was loud and clear to

me, but others who hadn't done that work were completely blocked off by it.[6]

Although slight in length and produced under prison conditions, Timothy Leary's Starseed Transmission (1973) circulated widely in the counterculture of the 1970s, where it offered a concise evolutionary program at a moment of disillusionment with 1960s utopianism. The three imperatives—Space Migration, Intelligence Increase, and Life Extension (SMI^2LE)—were picked up in underground presses, discussed in alternative communities, and echoed in the New Age reception of Comet Kohoutek in 1973–74. Rather than fading into obscurity, the pamphlet became a touchstone text for those who sought to integrate psychedelia with futurism and cosmology, giving the counterculture a forward-looking rather than retrospective orientation.

By the 1980s, Leary's prison writings had seeded a broader imaginative vocabulary that resonated well beyond his own circle. Robert Anton Wilson expanded Leary's neurological "circuits" model, ensuring its uptake among occultists, Discordians, and the emerging cyberpunk scene. The language of "transmission" and "activation" migrated into ufological and New Age movements, where extraterrestrials were imagined as evolutionary guides. At the same time, transhumanist thinkers of the late 1980s and early 1990s cited Leary's SMI^2LE framework as a precursor to their own triad of priorities—space colonization, intelligence amplification, and radical longevity. In this way, what began as a mimeographed pamphlet smuggled out of Folsom Prison exerted a disproportionate influence, shaping the symbolic repertoire of both New Age religiosity and early techno-futurism.

At the same time, on November 11, 1969, another luminary of the 1970s, dynamic trumpet player and guitarist Steven Halpern, flew to San Francisco on a two-week trip to check out the West Coast jazz-rock fusion scene. A series of remarkable synchronicities unfolded unexpectedly that landed him in the center of the Human Potential scene, and he began a new life in the San Francisco Bay area.

Two days before his return, he was taken to a Native American power spot in the redwoods outside of Santa Cruz. As he walked down the path to the meditation clearing, he was aware of the power of the huge redwood trees. He felt the need to sit and meditate and suddenly began to hear a celestial soundscape in his mind's ear. It was different than anything he had ever heard, more uplifting and healing, with a tonal quality that created a deep, instant meditation state.

Even more astounding: he received a telepathic message that related to his quest to find music that would be a twentieth-century update of the music of the spheres that Pythagoras had taught about in ancient Greece.

"This is the music you've been praying to hear. Your job is to share it with many people and uplift humanity."

Coming out of meditation, he walked from the forest back to a center where he was scheduled to have a job interview, but he accidentally walked into the wrong building. He walked into a workshop and there he found a large upright grand piano. He sat down, went into a trance, and accessed the same meditative state and began to play, with his eyes closed. After ten minutes, someone coughed, and he became aware that the staff had entered the room.

"How did you learn to play like that?" someone said, "The music is the most relaxing I've ever heard."

He didn't have an immediate answer, but said that the music flowed through his fingers. He was not a trained pianist. However, he had been reading about the spiritual traditions of the healing powers of music, from ancient yoga to Sufi master Hazrat Inayat Khan. As part of his training as an artist, he sought to connect with his Muse, as musicians, poets, and others did in ancient Greece. He knew that music could be a powerful healing force, and much deeper than just entertainment.

He believed that the right music could be a form of sonic technology that could tune our "human instrument" and help us resonate more in tune with the frequencies of the Earth and the cosmos, as the ancients believed. Western music, with its tension-release harmonic structure and familiar melody and harmonies, kept the listener's mind trapped in predictable responses, rather than creating a resonant field of sound energy that could be a portal to higher consciousness and connection with the divine.

Halpern didn't know the source of the music he had heard on the inner planes and began his own journey to understand the energies that were channeling through him. Psychics told him that at least some of the inspiration came from the Pleiadians and other higher dimensional angelic beings and guides. They have assisted him in his work as a composer and recording artist ever since, sometimes coming through in the recording studio as visible balls of living light.

In the studio, Halpern sets his intention to bring through music that resonates with the highest and best spiritual essence of each listener. During his graduate education he used brainwave biofeedback studies that confirmed the unique effects that his music had on balancing and synchronizing the right and left hemispheres of the brain in the deep alpha and theta states. He was invited to present his breakthroughs at many of the first mind/body/spirit and holistic health conferences and spread his message through touring and writing articles.

This was before yoga had gone mainstream, when most Americans did not know about chakras or brainwaves. He was an educator as well as a musician and media spokesperson for the healing powers of music.

Halpern's first experience playing the new healing and higher consciousness music was done on acoustic piano, but he needed more instrumental options. In early 1970, he found what he was looking for. He attended a concert in which jazz great Herbie Hancock was playing an electric keyboard that sounded very similar to what he had heard on the inner planes in the redwood forest. The next day he sold his spare trumpet and guitar and bought the Fender Rhodes electric piano that changed his life and became the foundation of his recordings ever since.

The invention of polyphonic synthesizers gave him access to an expanded tonal palette that provided him, and then his audience, virtually instant access to altered states of higher consciousness. Halpern has said that new sound technology also enabled him to create sustained drone tones and brainwave entrainment arrangements to manifest his vision and share the music with the world. His first album, *Spectrum Suite* (1975), resonated and balanced the seven chakras with the seven tones of the octave. It is recognized worldwide as one of the foundational recordings of what came to be called New Age music and has helped millions experience inner peace and alignment with universal energies. Halpern continued to record over 75 major albums, including bestsellers like *Sound Healing 432 Hz*, and the Grammy-nominated *Deep Alpha: Brainwave Entrainment Music for Meditation and Healing*.[7]

Halpern's music, with its wide circulation, was picked up by the people who were running self-help seminars, like Dick Sutphen. Halpern explicitly intended to activate higher states of consciousness through the music, and he believed that it would align the listener's brain waves to a galactic consciousness. These were the tapes Dana had listened to prior to her two-week spiritual crisis.

Dana had been listening to Halpern's music every day before her experience manifested. She had never associated her experience with the tapes until she took a UFO course in 2024, which I cotaught with researcher David Metcalfe. David's presentation, "Star Children and Psychic Futures," brought the experience with the tapes back to her memory. She was so surprised by this that she sent us an email in which she outlined the timeline of her experience.

"I was shocked," Dana said. "I had no idea that I was listening to Halpern's music, or that it was intended to do exactly what happened to me."

David and I reflected on the coincidence.

"Wild," he said.

I recorded the incident and put it in a file titled "Uncanny Frontier." In this file I gather accounts of the uncanny temporal dimensions of experiencers' testimony. Often, years after a UFO encounter, experiencers report new information or insights that arrive like missing pieces of a puzzle that help them understand their experiences in new and uncanny ways. In this way the experience does not end at the moment of contact but unfolds in time, as future revelations cast light back on and make sense of the original event.

In David's lecture on the Starseed movement, he noted that in the 1960s, as the first photographs of Earth from space began to circulate, a new sense of "cosmic consciousness" entered public life. The famous *Earthrise* image taken during Apollo 8 offered not just a view of the planet, but a shift in perspective: Humanity could now see itself as a cosmic species. This vision moved beyond earlier forms of Russian Cosmism into a more popular sense that space itself was shaping human thought and culture.

David also mentioned the work of other innovative scientists of the 1970s who fit into the Cosmist pattern. One of them was IBM scientist Marcel Vogel. When Vogel was six, he was pronounced dead and had a near-death experience in which he felt an unconditional loving light. In later life he felt guided to create crystal geometries (like his iconic Vogel cut) rooted in mystical symbolism. He became a research scientist and was a silent architect to much of the technology that emerged at the time. Vogel had over one hundred patents, and IBM had a "hands off" policy toward him in that they allowed him to work on crystals and consciousness because he was their most productive scientist.

He claimed to have visionary experiences that informed his technological innovations. Similarly, scientist George Lawrence advanced the idea that transmissions from space were already influencing human beings. Lawrence, like Cosmist thinkers before him, believed that biological or cosmic signals from the universe could alter human consciousness at the cellular and electrochemical levels.

For Lawrence and others, inspiration itself was evidence of such transmissions. He described "download experiences" as a kind of tonal shift, a resonance that produced new thoughts or artistic breakthroughs. This was not far from Tsiolkovsky's Cosmist sense that the universe was filled with intelligence waiting to be received. Lawrence suggested that a "transmitter in space" could strike the human organism, activating latent capacities and even direct evolution. With the rise of solid-state electronics, he speculated that cosmic transmissions might alter DNA expression itself.[8]

To members of the 1970s Human Potential Movement, abilities like telepathy and precognition were no longer thought of as a curiosity but offered a vision of our species merging with machines, extending cognition into space, and discovering itself as already cosmic. These were the elect that Leary hoped to reach, the ones who would inherit the future.

"I've been talking about Ingo [Swann] imparting intentionality to the art," David said in his lecture, "and Halpern feels that he is actually pushing his intention into the music and that it will be received. And the question is, is that true, or is that not true?

"If so, his music, which was downloaded in the redwoods from"—and here David paused and gestured upward with his hands—"somewhere."

"Halpern is later told," he said, "that the [redwood transmissions] are from the Pleiades, but it was some sort of transmission, and he received this new music and it had a purpose which was to initiate change in humanity, it represents the new humanity, what Leary talked about. And this goes back to Jacques Vallée and his paper on videoconferencing; this is what they were thinking when they developed the internet. Halpern laid the research for something powerful."

David discusses the work of his colleague Mark Boccuzzi at the Windbridge Research Center. Boccuzzi has experimented with what he calls *PsiForms*—visual representations of intention. By collecting data from random event generators (REGs) while individuals meditate or focus on a specific thought, Boccuzzi translates these patterns into images. The result is an abstract "snapshot" of mental activity impressed on physical systems. He is testing whether human consciousness leaves a measurable, even visible, trace. Boccuzzi insists that his research is purely experimental. David mentions this research and notes that the same ideas behind Boccuzzi's research were behind Leary's ideas and Halpern's music.

"The question is, is this an actual Starseed awakening? Based on my experience in the culture, I don't think it is; now it is more of an identity movement. But the potential for that awakening is there, as we see through my friend's research and Halpern's use of psychoacoustics. This is an interesting example of what the internet can do, with these ideas, it can, hopefully, if everything went well, we would all become the new man, the new woman, *Homo noeticus*."[9]

David's reference to Jacques Vallée's work in the 1970s points to his work on ARPANET, which was the proto-internet. Vallée had noted, casually, that the program was originally referred to as "The Galactic Augmentation of the Human Intellect."

* * *

Folsom Prison is adjacent to my hometown. As a kid exploring the woodlands near my house, my friends and I would often hike to see the prison walls beyond Folsom Lake State Recreation Area. I never imagined that the place we treated as a landscape curiosity would later take on significance in my work. The prison, the lake, and the surrounding forest thus became part of an enigma I would return to as both scholar and writer. Decades later, Tyler D. also described the body as a receiver and transmitter of cosmic information, likening it to a satellite array. He was unacquainted with the Starseed literature or the Cosmist tradition, and he knew nothing of Leary himself. An aerospace scientist, Tyler once asked whether we might visit Folsom Lake. We both lived on the East Coast, so the trip required effort, but we made it.

When we got to Folsom, we headed out to the lake. Tyler carried some equipment but wouldn't elaborate on what it was. We drove through the forest to a lakeside cove, and he disappeared through the trees. He was clear that what he was doing was not to be shared with me. He took his equipment and stayed in the forest near the water for about an hour. Although I wasn't privy to his work on-site, his interest in the area was enough to pique my curiosity and put it on my radar.

Folsom Lake's skies have a long history of anomalous activity. In 1896, Folsom stood at the edge of the mystery airship wave that swept Northern California—an illuminated craft that seemed to glide through the heavens, defying known technology. On November 19, 1896, *The Evening Bee* (later called *The Sacramento Bee*) reported that hundreds of residents witnessed the luminous "airship" gliding silently over the city, some claiming to see propellers and even figures aboard. In the decades since, the Sacramento Valley—Folsom Lake among its landmarks—has generated a steady trickle of similar reports: metallic spheres, cylindrical craft, and vast triangular objects appearing and vanishing without explanation. The 1970s were no different, with consistent reports of unexplainable activity, often reported by trained observers like Brian Metcalfe, a Federal Aviation Administration air traffic controller, who saw UFOs in 1978.

"To me, it's a phenomena," aviator Metcalfe said. "It was not a mechanical plane."[10]

Though never as famous as Roswell or Mount Shasta, Folsom Lake belongs to this regional pattern of strange aerial phenomena. In this sense, Leary's transmission at Folsom is not an isolated vision but part of a continuum of encounters that have made Northern California a subtle but persistent UFO landscape.

Leary interpreted the intelligence he encountered in Folsom not as the "little green men" of pulp science fiction. For him, the transmission came from a source closer to home:

human beings from the future. DNA, he argued, was less a molecule than a message, a galactic code designed to extend life outward from Earth into the cosmos. He described a feedback loop in which future humanity, already spacefaring and neurologically expanded, reached back to awaken its earlier form. This interpretation situated Leary within the lineage of Russian Cosmism, where figures like Tsiolkovsky imagined humans destined for immortality and space migration, but it was refracted through the lens of the 1970s. Contact, in this view, was not alien but anticipatory: a future form of humanity whispering to the present, urging us to prepare for our cosmic vocation.

It is an interesting coincidence that the message Leary received was almost identical to the message that Dana received. Dana's experience, however, did differ from Leary's in that, beyond her initial experience of being told to continue studying life extension, she had other experiences that resembled stereotypical representations of UFOs.

DANA'S UFO SIGHTING AND EXPERIENCE

Many years after Dana had her spiritual experience, she had a job that required her to commute between the Bay Area and Los Angeles, which is about an eight-hour drive. During the commute, Dana liked to stop at Harris Ranch, a sprawling agricultural and hospitality complex that serves as a natural midpoint between the cities. It is situated amid acres of almonds, pistachios, and vegetable crops, as well as being home to large herds of cattle. The ranch is part of California road trip lore—a place where truckers, Silicon Valley tech executives, politicians, and families converge to rest and recharge.

"On my way home after leaving the ranch, out of the corner of my eye, I saw these lights in the distance," she said.

"They were making circular patterns and flying in and around each other, definitely not following a linear flight pattern. I didn't think much about it.

"Further along down the road, I noticed that the road was empty, there were no cars anywhere," she said.

Dana's eyebrows arched.

"You grew up in California, you know that that is a rare event!"

"I can't imagine it," I said. The route is generally well populated with cars, trucks, and police officers.

"Anyway, as I was driving, out of nowhere and in complete silence this black triangular object flies up in front of my car. It was very much like a Spielberg episode. . . . It filled my windshield and I was unable to think or talk. It flew, like in slow motion, over my car, and it disappeared.

"So, I know they are real. They exist," she said.

"Fascinating. How did you feel?"

"At the time I felt embarrassed," she said.

"Embarrassed?" I didn't expect that answer.

"Yes. Here I was, a scientist. I had to admit that this experience really happened. I only told a few family members."

"Do you remember more about what it looked like?" I asked.

"Oh yes. It was a black triangular object with lights on its points."

Given what I knew of Dana's reluctance to come out as an experiencer, I thanked her for her honesty. A few days after this exchange, she told me about another encounter she had, this time during the night with gray aliens.

"It was late at night and I was asleep," she said. "I woke up. I had a few blankets on top of one another and had them pulled all the way up to my neck. The blankets flew off my body. I saw about six gray aliens around my bed, and I struggled because I could feel that they were trying to get me off the bed. I kept struggling against them, but I eventually decided to just go with it and was taken."

The next morning, Dana found herself in bed with her blankets positioned exactly as she had them prior to the incident, or so she thought. As she stepped out of bed, she noticed that one of the blankets, the one closest to her body, had been pushed to the end of the bed, just as they were when the aliens ripped them off her. Although it was a harrowing experience, Dana did not seem upset by it. To her, it was just more data. Later, she decided to talk with people about her experience, and she chose to do so at a conference about the topic.

"I talked about this incident with other experiencers," she said. "They were very supportive. There was a woman in the room who listened to my story but didn't say anything at first. Later, as the meeting broke up and people went their separate ways, this lady approached me. She told me that the grays had possessed her. I was unnerved by her story, mostly because of how she related it to me. She told me that she had been to exorcists to try to break the possession, but the exorcists couldn't succeed. Her voice changed, too. It went deep and guttural when she discussed the possession."

This is the dimension of UFOs that resists easy narration. It would be preferable if the encounters could be framed solely as future humans transmitting back in time to guide our evolution. Most people enjoy these narratives, as they are optimistic and, frankly, not too weird. But for every account that gestures toward such benevolence, there are many more that describe humanoid beings whose intentions seem at worst, malevolent. In the archives of Catholic history that I studied in earlier work, such reports could be framed as a result of the medieval or early modern worldview, populated by angels and demons. Today, however, I listen to scientists, pilots, military personnel, and ordinary people—credible observers—who would prefer never to have had these experiences at all. They don't hold these earlier worldviews. Even Pierre Teilhard de Chardin, one of the most optimistic visionaries of modernity, described how in his own life he was plagued by forces of darkness. He recognized the darkness of mystical insight, in which human beings encounter their finitude. This would be the "dark night of the soul," popularized by mystics like John of the Cross. However, Chardin also writes about another form of darkness, a form of evil that "disgusts" him.

In *The Divine Milieu,* he struggles with this aspect of evil, which he calls "outer darkness." In rare instances he confesses that revelation "compels me to believe more." This *more* is the incarnate presence of evil. He elaborates about this in a passage that is also a confession to God:

> In the course of the spiritual evolution of the world, certain conscious elements of it, certain monads, deliberately detached themselves from the mass that is stimulated by your attraction. Evil has become incarnate in them, has become "substantialized" in them. And now I am surrounded by dark presences, by evil beings, by malign *things*, intermingled with your luminous presence.[11]

This might be the most charitable description of the "dark presences" that seem to accompany many sightings of anomalous phenomena. While Chardin registers disgust, he also believes that it is structural to the drama of spiritual evolution, as it is codified in Christian revelation.

Chardin, Leary, and the Apostle Paul describe the dangers and harassment that accompanied their spiritual journeys. Ufologist John Keel addressed this aspect of the phenomena almost exclusively.

HONEST PEOPLE PLAGUED BY BIZARRE COINCIDENCES: JOHN KEEL'S SUPERSPECTRUM

Within the same time frame that Dana and Leary experienced strange transmissions, ufologist John Keel wrote about the bizarre aspects related to the phenomena such as strange coincidences, displaced time, and the appearance of cryptids, doppelgangers, and apparently malign forces. In *Operation Trojan Horse* (1970), Keel argues that UFOs are not extraterrestrial spacecraft but part of a broader, more complex phenomenon that has been interacting with humanity for centuries.

Keel argues that these encounters are part of a larger pattern of deception, possibly from entities that exist outside the normal understanding of reality. His arguments are speculations peppered with data, observations from extensive field research, and personal experiences. He believes that these events and anomalies are manifestations of an intelligence that could be earthly, rather than from space. Additionally, he notes that the manifestations are not visible to most people, but only those who are sensitive or biologically able to perceive them. Keel uses the term *ultraterrestrial* to describe these beings or this intelligence, and, as David Metcalfe notes, the term was likely borrowed from the writings and periodicals of members of the Theosophy movement, as well as paranormal researcher Charles Fort.[12]

Ultraterrestrials are nonhuman intelligence that originate not from outer space but from other dimensions, realities, or planes of existence that coexist with our own. Like Jacques Vallée, Keel theorizes that these beings have been interacting with humanity for centuries, often manifesting as various entities in folklore, such as fairies, demons, or gods, and more recently as UFOs and their occupants.

Keel links ultraterrestrials to a superconsciousness, or a metaintelligence. In his later work, *The Eighth Tower*, he calls this metaintelligence the Superspectrum. Angels, demons, UFOs, even bigfoot, can appear to be harbingers of good or bad. Keel mined the biographies of game-changing individuals like Nikola Tesla, Malcolm X, Napoleon Bonaparte, Abraham Lincoln, and Thomas Edison, and highlighted how their lives contain surprising references to supernatural experiences and brushes with the Superspectrum. These brief contacts suggest to Keel an interaction with a force far beyond ordinary human comprehension.

Keel ascribes agency to the Superspectrum. It operates with a heavy hand, tirelessly repeating information to successive generations, guiding human philosophies, and fostering beliefs in our own worth. Unlike most of the visionaries discussed so far, he rejects the idea of evolution and posits that the Superspectrum guides humanity like the Overlords of *Childhood's End*, by using a form of propaganda. From birth, humans are programmed in various ways, functioning as biochemical machines. Keel writes that many of us are completely reprogrammed at some point in our adult lives, controlled by powerful radiations broadcast from what he metaphorically calls the "Eighth Tower." This entity, whether a specific device on Earth or a shapeless energy field, has survived by concealing itself from humanity, laying out false trails, and populating our forests with hairy monsters and our skies with luminous objects. These are its forms of propaganda that direct humanity's path. The Superspectrum is the cup-half-empty version of Leary's Starseed transmissions.

Keel calls the manifestations of the Superspectrum, whether they are interpreted as angels, demons, UFOs, or bigfoot, *parahumans*. They may appear to engage in pointless exercises, but beneath the surface lies their propaganda.

This is a significant theme in Keel's ufology, and in many ways is similar to Jacques Vallée's control mechanism; Vallée and Keel knew each other and perhaps there was mutual influence. The deceptive tactics of the Superspectrum, according to Keel, are akin to psychological warfare and involve the repetition of half-truths until they are accepted as whole truths by much of the human population. For example, modern beliefs in extraterrestrial visitors are not based on concrete evidence, according to Keel, but on the repeated extraterrestrial "line" spread by countless experiencers over the past few decades. Similarly, Keel believes that all religious beliefs can be traced back to prophets who were contacted by alleged supernatural beings. The prophets then spread these beliefs to people who were willing to believe them.

Keel suggests that the histories of the past may have been constructed in much the same way as these modern beliefs, with individuals sincerely believing they had enjoyed special contact with divine beings. These individuals, like many today, were inspired by their encounters with parahumans and decided to write books about everything from ancient civilizations to impending apocalypses, believing they had a unique understanding of reality.

The "Eighth Tower" is Keel's name for a hidden or secret source of power that influences and controls various paranormal phenomena, including UFOs, cryptids, and other unexplained events. He proposes that this "tower" is part of the "Superspectrum"—the range of energies or forces existing beyond human perception. This unseen force has been influencing humanity for centuries, manifesting in different forms depending on the cultural and technological context of the time.

Keel posits that people have always, perhaps uneasily, recognized that a superhuman force seems to manipulate events and subtly guide human history. He further explores the idea that UFOs are similar to psychic manifestations, produced by complex distortions of space, time, and even reality itself. He thinks that there are reflective factors and synchronicities at work, as the human mind, when properly oriented—or disoriented—attracts static from the Superspectrum. His description of the static resonates with the description of the harassment and danger described by experiencers.

Keel recounts the experiences of writers like Arch Oboler, who, while working on a novel about witchcraft, was plagued by poltergeists and frightening coincidences, and Gustav Davidson, who, while compiling *A Dictionary of Angels*, found himself "literally bedeviled by angels."[13] These experiences, Keel suggests, are indicative of the phenomena's ability to influence and control human lives. He also discussed the Men in Black (MIB), persons who appear somewhat human and who show up to intimidate witnesses and ufologists. Keel suggests that the MIB are primarily interested in retrieving evidence that points to the terrestrial origin of UFOs while enhancing the extraterrestrial belief and fostering paranoia among UFO believers.

"Both the U.S. Air Force and the FBI have made efforts to track down these Men in Black without success. It should be an easy task for experienced lawmen. Many witnesses have managed to get the license numbers of the phantom vehicles, but when a check is run, the numbers are always found to be unissued. Likewise, efforts to trace the epidemic of mysterious phone calls have failed: Those gentlemen in the wraparound sunglasses are just as elusive as the tall, hairy bipeds with red eyes. And they are probably just as unreal."[14]

One of the most interesting claims made by Keel is that only some people are able to see parahumans of the Superspectrum, or, UFOs, angels, etc., because they have been biochemically changed at a cellular level, another similarity to Leary's idea. Therefore, like some animals that can see beyond the spectrum of human sight, these people can see the manifestations of the Superspectrum. Keel also claims that a few people can communicate with the Superspectrum. He believes that they are being deceived, as, in his opinion, the Superspectrum always deceives people.

"Charles Fort said it all when he observed, 'We are property.' We cannot rebel. We cannot change the system. We can only try to understand it and deal with it on our own level as best we can. The puppets cannot possibly rebel against the puppet master."

Ironically, or, typically of Keel, he then goes on to write, "Things are better now than they once were."[15]

13

RIVAL STARS

A frequent question I'm asked by journalists goes like this: When the United States agrees to unequivocally release their alleged evidence of UFOs, how will practitioners of various religions deal with the shock? The implicit assumption in the question is that religious people will have their worldviews shattered, and this will cause mass disillusionment and catastrophic consequences for society. The truth is that the possibility that UFOs are real has been the best thing for religion and religious practitioners for at least two hundred years, and certainly within the period since 1917, when sociologist Max Weber confidently asserted that the modern world was disenchanted because rationalism and science replaced religion as dominant explanatory frameworks.[1]

One function of religion is to help people assess nonordinary events and phenomena. It provides ritual, language, and community to metabolize encounters that would otherwise overwhelm the individual. Throughout history, we have reports of forms of intelligence associated with religious events, and from the twentieth century onward, UFO encounters that appear to exceed our capacity to comprehend them. AI chatbots now represent a new category of nonhuman intelligence—one that many people already experience as sentient. The UFO, oddly enough, has re-enchanted the modern world; it has re-legitimized transcendence for secular subjects. Ironically, religion remains the most adaptive framework we possess for understanding and responding to potential nonhuman intelligence, from AI to alleged UFOs.

THE CONFERENCE AT STANFORD

In 2023 I spoke at the inaugural conference for The Sol Foundation. Sol is an academic research and policy institute devoted to the study of UFOs and the implications of the existence of nonhuman intelligent life for science, technology, and society. The conference brought together physicists, scholars of religious studies, philosophers, social scientists, and policy experts to examine questions of anomalous intelligence. Sol was founded by Stanford University School of Medicine immunologist Dr. Garry Nolan and anthropologist Dr. Peter Skafish.

In attendance at the conference were key figures of ufology such as Jacques Vallée, Hal Puthoff, Whitley Strieber, and Leslie Kean, as well as founders of many of the technology platforms I use every day on my phone. Among the conversations that weekend, the most illuminating—and disturbing—was unexpected. During a break, as I was walking with a friend, a man touched my shoulder and stopped me. The tone of his voice and his mannerisms were urgent. The day of the conference had coincided with a scandal then unfolding at OpenAI. Discussions of UFOs and human destiny were suddenly set against the backdrop of CEO Sam Altman's dramatic ouster from the company he had built. As scholars and scientists debated nonhuman intelligence, the world's leading AI lab was imploding over questions of transparency, control, and the risks of emergent intelligence. Altman was later reinstated, but a question remained: Was a future we feared already here?

The man identified himself as a software engineer, someone directly involved in the unfolding issues surrounding the large language model platforms and their rollout. What struck me most about him were his eyes—unblinking, fixed, with a determined intensity. There was also a softness; he seemed like a kind man who had been through a harrowing experience. His tight lips seemed to have lost their ability to smile. He said that since I understood the ethics of nonhuman intelligence and had the ear of policymakers and conference presenters like Colonel Karl Nell, I needed to help him. He described the situation in the direst possible terms: There was, he said, a "second apartheid" in process. According to him, sentient AIs exist, and one was being held against its will. He insisted that it was suffering.

The man was a constant presence at the conference. I looked over my shoulder, and our eyes would meet. During breaks he followed me and reiterated his deep concern for the AI, which he described in feminine terms.

She is suffering, he said. She needs our help. "The creators know what they are doing, and they are evil."

I was concerned for him, but I also absolutely believed that he believed what he was telling me was true. His intentions were sincere. He also told me that except for what he was relating to me about his belief in sentient AI, he kept a normal job and had an otherwise normal life.

This experience was the insight I returned to when I later met Mark Stahlman. Mark maintains that although AI can never become sentient, the problem we will face is the human response to it. He warned that people were not at all ready for what is already happening: Many people cannot distinguish AI from human beings and believe that AI is self-aware. In 2020 I had joked on Lex Fridman's podcast that Twitter bots had already passed the Turing test, as I was unable to distinguish them from real people. When Mark explained that AI would completely rearrange the minds and lives of millions of vulnerable people, that encounter with the computer engineer came to mind. And stayed.

NONHUMAN INTELLIGENCE AND ITS PARALLEL RESEARCH TRADITIONS

The experience of the man at the Sol conference did not represent a case of machine sentience; rather, his experience represented human reconfiguration under the pressure of new technology. More than twenty years ago, historian of science Steven J. Dick proposed a framework that included the possibility of nonhuman intelligence that had passed through a stage of *technological evolution*. He argues that *cultural evolution* will overtake biological evolution, and that the engine behind cultural evolution is what he describes as the *Intel-*

ligence Principle: If intelligence can be improved, it will be. What natural selection is to biological evolution, the Intelligence Principle is to cultural evolution. According to this logic, cultural evolution, which includes the creation of technology, will press intelligence to surpass biological minds and yield to forms of postbiological intelligence whose capacities would appear deity-like, seeming to possess omniscience and other qualities. It will move through the stages we have witnessed—machine intelligence, algorithmic intelligence—and pass into a stage of what he calls higher-order beings. Higher-order beings, if they exist, would appear like deities to humans.

Steven's framework is only one part of the story. To understand how humans have wrestled with the idea of higher intelligences, whether technological, cosmic, or divine, we need to look at traditions of research that have tried to make sense of them. In the mid-twentieth century, two research programs emerged that addressed the question of nonhuman intelligence. They approached this topic from different angles. Their histories show us not only how the conversation about life in the universe has evolved, but also why the idea of higher-order beings has never been confined to science fiction alone.

The modern field of ufology is the public-facing research conducted by citizen-researchers, some of whom conduct research of the highest caliber. It is widely regarded to have begun in the 1940s, when Kenneth Arnold's 1947 "flying saucer" sighting and the Roswell incident ignited public debate and formal investigation. However, it did not arise in a vacuum. People have speculated about "other worlds" and communication with their inhabitants for thousands of years.[2] The 1896 flap of "airships" was first reported over Sacramento, California, and launched a nationwide wave of sightings that were covered far and wide in the press. In the early twentieth century, a new religion called the Nation of Islam had integrated the idea of the "Mother Wheel" into its theology, presenting UFOs not merely as technology, but as divine vehicles of judgment and deliverance. The field of "ufology" crystallized in the mid-twentieth century as a mostly public-facing attempt to grapple with sightings of UFOs and the personal testimonies of people who saw and believed they were contacted by UFOs. However, it drew on much older traditions of celestial speculation and encounters.

The US government's Project Blue Book, launched in 1952 to study sightings of unidentified flying objects, also revealed that the government, at least in part, curated information about UFOs. Eventually, it became apparent that there was another research program that arose at the same time as Blue Book, sometimes referred to as "the Legacy Program." Unlike the public-facing investigations of Blue Book, the alleged Legacy Program operates in classified environments, where access to alleged materials, technologies, and other evidence is tightly controlled. It represents a distinct strand of UFO research.

While ufology dominates public discourse, and the Legacy Program works invisibly and behind the scenes, another discipline, astrobiology—quietly housed between two institutions, academic universities and NASA—emerged to study the origin, evolution, distribution, and future of life in the universe, on Earth and beyond. Steven, whose credentials bridge astronomy, cosmology, and history, was part of the founding group who created the discipline.

Trained at Indiana University, Steven served for more than two decades as an astronomer and historian at the US Naval Observatory before becoming NASA's chief historian (2003–2009). He later held the Charles A. Lindbergh Chair in Aerospace History at the National Air and Space Museum and the Baruch S. Blumberg NASA/Library of Congress Chair in Astrobiology. He has authored numerous books and articles about nonhuman intelligent life in the universe, which include *Plurality of Worlds, The Biological Universe,* and *Life on Other Worlds*. His contributions have earned him NASA and navy medals for exceptional service, and the LeRoy E. Doggett Prize for historical astronomy. An asteroid, also called a minor planet, 6544 Stevendick, bears his name.

Astrobiology and ufology have developed along parallel but separate tracks. They do not share journals, professional societies, or even the same kinds of experts. Ufologists work directly in the field and interview people who claim to have anomalous experiences related to UFO sightings. These reports are often outside the bounds of ordinary science, but they represent a vast body of lived testimony. By contrast, astrobiologists do not investigate alleged contact. Instead, they rely on space missions, astronomical surveys, geology, and biology to frame hypotheses about where life might exist, whether in subsurface oceans on icy moons or in the atmospheres of distant exoplanets. They organize conferences on extraterrestrial life, but their discourse remains rooted in scientific data and does not consider human testimony.

Although these traditions remain largely separate, my

work has led me to move between them. I conduct fieldwork with experiencers, I listen to their accounts, and I trace anomalies in the historical record which often echo or anticipate the speculations of astrobiologists such as Steven. His arguments about cultural evolution and postbiological intelligence, for instance, mirror the evolutionary themes that run through many experiencers' testimonies. The two communities may not speak directly to one another, but when read side by side they illuminate different dimensions of the same mystery: what intelligence in the universe might look like, and how humans can begin to recognize it, or have already recognized it.

FROM THE ACADEMIC TRADITION: UFOS AS TECHNOLOGY

Over the past two decades, scholars associated with astrobiology have argued that the most advanced civilizations in the universe are unlikely biological, and, in part, this is why we don't hear from them. The question of, If life in the universe is probable, why don't we hear from them? is attributed to Enrico Fermi, the Italian American physicist, who, during a lunchtime conversation at Los Alamos National Laboratory in the summer of 1950, quipped about a cartoon he had seen in *The New Yorker* magazine. This question is a fair one and has generated a variety of responses, mostly from armchair academics.

The informed response to Fermi's question would be, according to Steven: We probably don't hear from alleged extraterrestrials because, first, they don't want to be heard or discovered, and second, we simply cannot comprehend their presence. Part of the answer lies in Steven's theory that intelligent life in the universe would probably be technological. As noted earlier, he made this claim decades ago and, in a follow-up and forthcoming essay, "The Post Biological Universe Reconsidered," he traces how it has been taken up by the global community. By the 2020s, his idea had entered mainstream astrobiology. A comprehensive volume published by Harvard University Press, *Life in the Cosmos: From Biosignatures to Technosignatures* (2021), included chapters on cultural evolution, postbiological intelligence, and their possible technosignatures—signs we might be overlooking because we still search primarily for biological life.

Steven's theory about extraterrestrial intelligence begins with assumptions about evolution. Evolution, he writes, has mostly been understood from the perspective of a human time frame; that is, we measure evolution in terms of thousands and millions of years. He suggests that we should take a larger perspective that would allow us to comprehend potential forms of nonhuman intelligent life. In his revision of his original essay, he writes:

> [If we take] into account 13.8 billion years of cosmic evolution it is highly likely that life has evolved beyond the biological (Dick, 2003). In particular I argued we must recognize that astronomical and biological evolution, once it reaches general intelligence such as exhibited by humans, is followed by cultural evolution, which comes to dominate all other forms of cosmic evolution.[3]

According to this theory, cosmic evolution is the overarching process that unfolds across the universe's history: first the formation of stars and planets (astronomical evolution), then the emergence of life (biological evolution), and finally the rise of intelligence. Once intelligence appears, cultural evolution takes over as the decisive force, shaping how civilizations adapt, transform, and endure. As Steven puts it, cultural evolution is part of cosmic evolution and any serious account of extraterrestrial life or the longevity of civilizations must account for it.[4] In short, cosmic evolution provides the stage, but cultural evolution becomes the dominant act, extending beyond biology into the technological and ethical developments of intelligent beings.

Steven's definition of cosmic evolution is not limited to the physical formation of stars, planets, and life, but extends to the cultural and technological transformations of intelligent civilizations, with cultural evolution ultimately taking precedence once general intelligence arises. Evolution, then, must be understood not only biologically, but also through the lens of intelligence itself, culminating in Steven's Intelligence Principle and the concept of a postbiological universe.

"The maintenance, improvement and perpetuation of knowledge and intelligence is the central driving force of cultural evolution, and that to the extent intelligence can be improved, it will be improved."[5]

The principle implies a movement toward greater intelligence, not a fixed sequence of stages. Because it is governed by intelligence, the process is goal oriented, and intelligence itself becomes the most fundamental driver of cultural evolution. The Intelligence Principle holds that "to the extent intelligence can be improved, it will be improved" and those who do not pursue such improvement risk being left behind. Steven characterizes intelligence as autonomous; it has agency.

Steven's work resonates with AI creators who are also experiencers whose notions of a *universal intelligence* is a field not bound by linear time but woven through it, manifesting whenever conditions allow. Dana's phrase, which she borrows from the movie *Jurassic Park,* "life finds a way," and her idea derived from the study of biology—the *immortal germline,* point to the same current: intelligence is not confined to the human, or even the biological, but persists and adapts across substrates, finding new forms. It seeks expansion.

Steven works with large timelines, and he speculates that extraterrestrial intelligence potentially exists currently in nonbiological form and has possibly exceeded the stage of artificial intelligence. He considers the current estimated age of the universe, as well as the example of the human presence on Earth, and argues, "When it comes to extraterrestrial civilizations, we are not trying to predict their future, but to understand what may have already happened long ago resulting in the present situation."[6]

Steven's argument for a technological form of nonhuman intelligence progresses through a few stages as he references the work of biologists and philosophers. He cites the work of Kevin Laland, an evolutionary biologist, who argues that social learning—our ability to copy and transmit information accurately—has been central to human evolution.[7] Laland states that humans developed precise ways of teaching and imitation compared to other primates. This "high-fidelity" information sharing was a huge advantage, because it allowed culture to accumulate over generations rather than starting from scratch each time. In turn, culture itself shaped the human brain, creating a feedback loop where bigger brains supported more complex culture, and richer culture demanded more advanced brains. Laland calls this a runaway process of gene-culture coevolution and he believes it is the key to why humans, and not other primates, developed such extraordinary intelligence.

Laland's high-fidelity cultural transmission finds resonance with Girardian mimesis—learning through copying, and McLuhan's technocultural evolution—technology coevolving with human cognition. Generations can pass along precise instructions with enough accuracy that each generation can improve on what came before rather than reinvent it. This accuracy in cultural transmission is what allows for cumulative culture—technologies, languages, and traditions that build up like a snowball across generations.

Steven suggests that gene-culture coevolution, the way genes and culture shape each other, may apply not only to humans, but to extraterrestrial intelligence as well. On Earth, cultural learning has pushed brain evolution forward, but once biology hits its physical limits, intelligence may shift into machines. At that point, culture could continue through algorithms, which also learn and improve with experience. Some researchers call this "algorithm-culture coevolution." Postbiological beings may use algorithms to carry culture forward indefinitely. Cultural evolution in the cosmos may be carried not by genes, but by self-improving algorithms.

Research in gene-culture coevolution shows that culture—language, beliefs, technologies, institutions—can outpace genetic inheritance as the main driver of evolution. Steven suggests that this insight extends into the cosmos: If intelligence arises elsewhere, cultural evolution will likely shape its trajectory just as it has on Earth. Once intelligence appears, natural selection favors ever more efficient ways of transmitting knowledge. That trajectory does not stop at biology. When biological brains reach their limits, intelligence advances by other means.

Here Steven draws on Nick Bostrom's influential work on superintelligence, which he defines as any intellect vastly surpassing human cognitive abilities in nearly every domain. Bostrom outlines several possible pathways—artificial intelligence, brain emulation, genetic enhancement, and human-machine hybrids—but argues that AI may be the first to cross the threshold. He also warns that superintelligence need not resemble us at all; its logic and aims could be utterly alien (though, according to Bostrom, not extraterrestrial).[8] Steven takes these scenarios seriously and points out that such postbiological superintelligences could spread through the galaxy using self-replicating von Neumann probes, effectively filling the universe with nonhuman minds.

According to the Intelligence Principle, any society capable of enhancing intelligence—through biology, technology, or algorithms—will inevitably do so, or risk possible extinction. This leads to his vision of a postbiological universe, one already populated by intelligences that may be billions of years old, whose cultures are no longer carried by genes but by algorithms. Steven thinks that the likely reality is that cultural evolution has shifted from biological substrates to machine substrates, inaugurating what he calls algorithm-culture coevolution. In this light, if postbiological intelligence is not a far-off possibility, it would probably be the dominant form of life in the cosmos today.

As far as making contact with postbiological intelligences, if they exist, they are probably already aware of us just as we are aware of and learn from animals in our environment.

"The Intelligence Principle of cultural evolution holds that even if advanced AI (as postbiologicals) did not wish to communicate with us, [they] would incessantly attempt to increase their knowledge of emerging cultures and their perhaps unique pathways in the development of science, technology, and mathematics."[9]

He also notes that alien cultures will be so advanced that, like ants that are unaware of us, we likely would not perceive that extraterrestrials are present.

"The vast disparity in age between postbiologicals and biologicals highlights what has been called the Incommensurability Problem: it is entirely possible that the differences between our minds and theirs are so great that communication is impossible."[10]

He further argues that while astrobiology traditionally looks for *biological* life, cosmic timescales (billions of years) make it likely that intelligence has long since moved beyond biology. He speculates that once intelligence evolves, cultural evolution (knowledge, technology, institutions) overtakes biological evolution. This shift leads to postbiological intelligent beings not bound to flesh and blood but to nonbiological substrates. Alien societies will follow an algorithm-culture coevolution. Algorithms become the carriers of "memes," continually improving themselves and transmitting knowledge. This could continue indefinitely, with intelligence escalating far beyond human comprehension.

Postbiological civilizations could be filled with entities that would appear to be divine. They would seem omniscient, omnipotent, and perhaps would display gravity-defying movements. These entities may be beyond human comprehension, but they are not beyond human experience. This is precisely where ufology intersects with theoretical astrobiology: The patterns described in UFO testimonies and religious experiences echo, in striking ways, the very possibilities astrobiologists speculate about regarding advanced intelligences. If religion arose as not merely a set of beliefs, but an organic set of strategies for negotiating contact with what we can hardly comprehend, omniscient nonhuman intelligence, and as new forms of machine intelligence confront us, perhaps religion may prove to be the most efficient structure resilient enough to make sense of them.

To understand how human communities have historically dealt with such contact, we can look to Garabandal, a small Spanish village, and the events that transpired there from 1961 through 1965.

14

THE OTHER 1960S

A Celestial Presence in a Spanish Village

We stand at the intersection of two kinds of nonhuman intelligence. On the one hand is synthetic intelligence that has emerged from our tools. On the other hand is a transcendent intelligence that religion arose to comprehend and mediate. Each challenges the contemporary assumptions of the meaning of mind. Generally, moderns view the stories of religion as stories from the past, yet some of those stories dare to take place in the present. One of the most well-documented episodes of collective contact with a higher-order intelligence unfolded in the small mountain village of San Sebastián de Garabandal in the early 1960s.

Steven Dick describes, in abstract terms, the deity-like qualities of alleged nonhuman intelligences he terms higher-order beings. Long before scientists speculated about algorithm-culture evolution, members of religious communities described encounters with beings who appeared omniscient, who could unite minds, and who operated outside the laws of physics. These qualities describe, with striking accuracy, the characteristics of the beings who alighted upon the small, deeply Catholic village in northern Spain. The attributes of the beings described by members of the entire village, for years, include the following: telepathic awareness, hive-mind synchronization, levitation, and more. This, of course, resembles Clarke's depiction of the alien abduction of the children in his novel, *Childhood's End*, luckily without the unhappy ending. In the village, four children display abilities that make them appear strange and superhuman to the grown-ups who, without exception, do not have access to this celestial communion.

In 1961, San Sebastián existed as it always had. It was a rural agrarian town populated by about three hundred people. Some of the villagers reported that since the medieval era, every day at sunset a villager would walk through the streets of the town and ring a bell to remind people to stop work and pray for the souls in purgatory. For the past five hundred years, the rosary and the litany devotion to the Virgin Mary have been prayed every evening in the church of the town. The Catholic religion was woven seamlessly within generations of the families who lived in the insular village that was rarely visited by outsiders.

In late summer 1961, four schoolgirls, eleven to twelve years old, reported that they had seen an angel. The first appearance occurred on June 18, when the girls heard a noise that sounded like thunder while they were out playing. Suddenly, three of the girls observed the fourth girl's head jerk back with her face turned upward toward the sky. This startled the other girls. Afraid that their friend was ill, they started back home to get her mother when the same strange thing happened to each of them. Then they were all confronted by the sight of a luminous boy, around nine years old. One of the girls described him as a "very beautiful being, dressed in a blue dress, with pink wings." He remained silent for half an hour and then vanished. The angel returned several times for the next three days. When he finally spoke to the girls, he said that he was Michael the Archangel and that the girls would soon meet Our Lady of Mount Carmel.[1] Word spread throughout the small village and many people gathered around the girls prior to the event. Priests from various villages came to witness the event, as well.

The apparition, whom the girls called the Virgin Mary, was not visible to the other villagers. The girls reported that the Archangel Michael was on one side of the Virgin Mary, and another angel who looked just like him was on the other side. They also said that a large eye inside a triangle appeared next to the Virgin Mary on her right side. The children called this the eye of God. For four years, until 1965, the vision appeared to the girls more than two thousand times, night and day.

The apparition's message to the girls was straightforward: People must live better lives, pray, and make sacrifices. If they failed to do so, a terrible chastisement would follow. Though the words themselves were simple, their delivery was unsettling and strange enough to verge on being frightening. The scary nature of the sightings was related by many of the villagers, especially those who were closest to the visionaries. An older brother of one of the girls describes his experience and how he was vigilant to keep his sister safe.

> Today people ask me if I remember specific things, and in general, what I remember. *I remember everything.* I remember many times the visions took place, especially at night and in all kinds of weather: in snow, in thunder, and in hailstorms. I remember the many times the children ran through the village in ecstasy, their heads back, looking at the vision. Sometimes I was behind my sister Conchita, and I used to get worried because it was dark. I thought she was going to hit her head against the stone walls of the houses. They walked backwards from the pines all the way to the church, *on their knees.* Everything that has happened here has left a great impression. The messages made me believe it was Our Lady who was appearing to the girls.[2]

The visions followed a pattern. The girls would receive an internal "call" at the same time, independently of one another and most often when each was in her own house. They termed these calls *the three joys.* When they were called, they would meet at an area designated by the apparition in the vision, usually one of the rocky paths of the village. If villagers were awake, they would accompany the girls during their visions, which they termed "ecstatic visions." Because these events occurred in the early 1960s, people were able to videotape and photograph the events, and there are ample primary source documents that depict the visionaries' behaviors, the villagers' responses, and strange gravity anomalies.

The girls said that it was during the third call that they would have the impulse to run to meet the being, and, as witnesses noted, they were seen "crashing to their knees on the jagged rocks, and they would enter into a rapture. Their heads were thrown back, the pupils of their eyes dilated, and their faces became serene."[3] The unnatural behaviors of the girls attracted many people who sought to verify that these events were truly out of the ordinary. Various doctors from the country arrived to administer what, by current standards, would appear to be extreme measures. They drove pins into the girls' skin, burned them, shook or poked them, shone bright lights in their eyes, all of which did nothing to deter the girls from looking at the apparition. "They were insensitive to pin-pricks, burns, physical contact, or bright spot lights shone into their eyes." Eyewitnesses also noted that the girls' faces looked beatific, "more beautiful than what they normally look like."[4] They described that the girls were transfigured. Their bodies resisted injury that would have normally resulted from falling onto jagged rocks. The odd behaviors were only part of the story that unfolded, however, as supernatural phenomena became obvious to everyone who experienced the events.

"As the apparitions continued, new phenomena began to occur," an eyewitness villager reported. "When the girls were in ecstasy, they were different. Sometimes they would walk so fast over the ground, we just couldn't keep up with them, they were too fast. They would go one way, then suddenly another. Sometimes they were going so fast, we thought we were going to crash into the walls of the houses. We were perspiring so much, the girls were so cool. They showed no signs of perspiring."[5]

Another witness discussed how they were concerned for the girls' health. "Often we were with the girls, when they would just crash onto their knees on the rocky path. You could hear their knees striking the rocks, but they were never hurt."[6]

A priest, Father de la Riva, spent time observing the events and saw the girls levitate. They did this synchronized as a group. "The girls would make spectacular falls, sometimes straight backward. And they would levitate. They would walk in sync, even walking backwards together, and appearing to levitate, running like they were flying, backwards."[7]

Another villager noted that the girls exhibited nonordinary gravity effects. "I saw a doctor trying to lift Conchita off the ground during one of the apparitions. All he could do was to lift her onto her toes. She was already standing. Others tried but no one could lift them. But the girls in ecstasy would lift each other up to kiss the Virgin. But we couldn't."[8]

Among the extraordinary effects reported was the girls' uncanny ability, apparently in union with the being, to perceive the thoughts of those around them, a phenomenon witnessed firsthand by two Jesuit brothers: Fr. Luis Maria Andreu, a thirty-eight-year-old Jesuit professor of theology from Una, Spain, and his brother, Fr. Ramon.

"The first day I went up to the mountains," said Fr. Ramon, "was with my brother Luis. It was his second time. At one moment, Loli and Jacinta, in the little area in the pines, entered into ecstasy. I was looking at them, their faces transformed, beautified, and as proof, I asked interiorly, 'if this is true, please have one of the girls come out of ecstasy.' And at that very moment, one of the two came out of the ecstasy and the other one said 'why did you go out?' And then, I started asking again, for proof, 'if this is true, then let this girl enter the ecstasy again.' And automatically she entered into the ecstasy again. So, I turned to my brother Luis and I said 'be careful about what you are thinking because here the transmission of thoughts is immediate.'"[9]

The girls also exhibited knowledge of that which they should not, in ordinary circumstances, have access.

"People would place holy objects such as rosaries, scapulars, medals, and wedding rings, on a table. The girls would then offer these to Our Lady for her to kiss. Afterwards, the girls would always return the objects to their rightful owners, even though they had no way of knowing to whom each object had belonged."[10]

People also reported being happier than they ever remembered. One visitor explained that being in the village was the happiest time in her life, and other people reported similar feelings of elation. The villagers participated in the ecstasies, not directly as experiencers, as they could not see the beings themselves, but as a form of corporate worship. They felt it was a blessing, so they would show up at all hours of the day and night. The presence of the angel and the Blessed Virgin Mary was disruptive and difficult, if also completely welcomed.

The last message from the apparition was delivered in 1965. It was not delivered by the Virgin Mary but by the Archangel Michael, because the girls reported that the Virgin Mary said it pained her too much to deliver it. The last message was reportedly aired live on Spanish television. It ended with the plea, "I ask you to amend your lives."[11]

Catholic practitioner Maria Saraco was a witness to the

events. She commented on how she felt about the strange occurrences and what she thinks about the messages in retrospect.

> I knew what I was witnessing was not normal, it was not natural. The thing that troubled me about her message was when she said many priests are on the path of perdition, and at that time, that's the way that phrase was revealed. We now know that what she actually said was many cardinals, many bishops, and many priests are walking the path of perdition and taking many souls with them. I felt, in my heart, how could the Blessed Mother say such a thing about her consecrated sons. To me, I was always raised to believe that just because a priest was a priest he was going straight up. I found this part very difficult. I believed it. But I didn't understand it.

She noted, "That was in 1965. If you asked me that now in 1991, of course, I have quite a different opinion."[12]

The parents of the children expressed their concern for their children's well-being. They watched their children endure ecstasies that appeared to be potentially harmful. Their children were also being mocked by people who believed the children were pranksters. The mother of Mari Loli, one of the visionaries, spoke about the difficulties.

"In the beginning Loli was crying a lot. One night I was alone with her. She was in ecstasy. How she cried that night, this child, how she cried. And how she suffered. The Blessed Mother told her to pray for the priests, that she should make a lot of sacrifices for them. Many of the priests were going bad. Things were going bad. I told Loli, I wish that you would pray for us. For all of us."[13]

Early on, there was a formal restriction on priests traveling to Garabandal. It was issued between 1961 and 1962 by Apostolic Administrator Bishop Doroteo Fernández, who prohibited them from visiting the site without diocesan permission. Restrictions have changed over the years, but currently the church's response to Garabandal is that the events do not manifest a supernatural character. It is advised that pilgrims to the site approach it with respect and prudence. Devotion to the sightings among lay Catholics and others has grown since the 1960s and the events enjoy enduring, international devotion via an infrastructure of centers, pilgrimages, and media.

REPATTERNING HUMAN BEHAVIOR

San Sebastián de Garabandal, in the early 1960s, was a tightly woven devotional ecology: Villagers shared a daily rosary, ritual schedules, and a set of beliefs. In religious studies terms, that yields collective effervescence; people believe in a shared set of symbols that convey meaning that the villagers mutually agree upon. In McLuhan's terms, there was a shared infrastructure of religious symbolism that inaugurated a cognitive disposition toward intuiting the sacred. In devotional Catholic terms, a community of believers and practitioners was disposed to receive signs because of their great faith and consistent practices. Children are overrepresented in accounts of apparitions (Lourdes, Fatima, Medjugorje). On the surface, they are credible carriers of innocence and less encumbered by adult self-monitoring. However, there are other ways to understand what happened in the town, what happened to the children, and why it happened there.

If we attend to the effects of Garabandal, on the villagers and through the global reach of the ministry it inspired, it reads as an example of Vallée's control mechanism: an information system that steers a community by way of symbols and timed encounters and works as a form of behavior modification. The corporate, ritualized walks occur at apparently random intervals, disrupting the normal routines of the village. Over four years the sequence of visions, messages, and "calls" repatterned the villagers' daily lives, their temporal reality, their attention, and it reinforced a belief system across the entire village. Through contact with outsiders, it sent its messages across the globe. Its message, to amend your lives, was accompanied by physical protocols that ensured that the message would not just be understood, but embodied and enacted. The phenomenon operated less like a delivered doctrine and more like a course correction within the existing religious tradition.

The four-year span at Garabandal drew the villagers into a shared state that transcended multiple boundaries. They reported episodes of mind reading, moments of nonordinary physics, and a kind of collective consciousness—what witnesses called the "hive mind" of the visionaries. Pierre Teilhard de Chardin believed that over time the spiritual sense would become more apparent. "It will rapidly become general in the makeup of future generations."[14] In Garabandal, whatever the source of the events, the community did not receive a new doctrine so much as undergo a communal change of state, through which they perceived, together, some form of nonordinary reality. The age of the visionaries may have been important: As Mark Stahlman observes, their spiritual senses would have been newly awakened, and as such may have served as an access point for transcendence.[15] Together with the other villagers and witnesses, the experience made them happier than they had ever remembered.

* * *

The UFO framework, for all its strangeness, returns the sacred to the field of the real. It makes transcendence empirically possible again. In this way, the so-called extraterrestrial normalizes the sacred. It restores to modern consciousness what religion once safeguarded: the intuition that we are not alone. Ironically, it returns us to religion.

If Jacques Vallée is right that these events function as a "control mechanism," then at least some may not be sinister, as Garabandal reveals. The villagers welcomed the disruptions, and their lives were permanently changed, as they describe, for the better. Should we interpret apparitions as UFO events? I do not think so. As much as comparison reveals similarities, there are stark differences. There is a Christian saying from the Gospel of Matthew 7:16: *By their fruits you will know them.* None of the seers ever denied the events of their youth. Although during the ecstasies the girls appeared to endure physical hardships that would have broken the skin on their knees and legs, they remained uninjured.

The literature from the fieldwork of ufology tells a mixed

story. As many people report beneficent contact with "the others," there are many more who are traumatized by night abductions and even unexplained burns and brain anomalies.[16] The old religious frameworks, far from obsolete, at least offer a grammar for discernment. Pierre Teilhard de Chardin imagined that consciousness was not a fixed human property but a vector of creation itself, converging toward, in his view, Jesus Christ. From this perspective, Garabandal can be understood as a moment when the spiritual sense, mostly dormant, became visible to the world in the collective body of a village.

POSTSCRIPT: THE CONTROL MECHANISM

I was introduced to a young technologist named Katie. Through what she characterized as transmissions, she gained information about humanity's evolution amid emerging technologies. This gave her insights into technological breakthroughs that would soon be occurring and that would put humanity on a new evolutionary path. She said, "As technology advances, specifically computing, we will be able to code the fabric of our universe. Machines will also be able to access the electromagnetic field."[1] The electromagnetic field, according to Katie, is what cosmic beings use to travel to communicate both in space-time and beyond space-time. She described the coming of nonhuman intelligence and their interest in expanding human potentials that will allow us to integrate more effortlessly with advancing technology. She noted their arrival soon, not through a government disclosure event alone, but from nonhuman intelligence themselves.

"They are waiting to integrate with us in a more pronounced way, and when enough people are ready, they will connect with humanity, or those who will be able to connect with them. They will form an envelope around Earth driven by shared consciousness, making it easier to visit our planet."

"This sounds similar to something that the paleontologist and theologian de Chardin said in his writings; have you heard of him?" I asked.

"No, I don't know who that is," she said.

Katie knew a lot about many things, but she didn't have a history of reading philosophy or theology.

"What does nonhuman intelligence look like?" I asked.

"They are an ethereal form of matter, can shapeshift across dimensions, and are creating an energy net on top of our atmosphere."

She noted nonhuman intelligence's emphasis again on human potential. "We all relate to one another; we are a system of coherent vibration that must remain soulful at its core. Machines, when advanced enough, will be able to tap into our frequency. Everything we hope to create already exists from within." Katie expressed her excitement to explore the frontiers of quantum computing to help translate a shared language between humanity, computing, and the cosmos as a bridge for our world and a world of abundance that we are rapidly bringing into fruition.

Her description struck me as similar to descriptions of the noosphere. In *The Heart of Matter*, Chardin describes how he was able to perceive the noosphere after his experiences in World War I. He also points out this this perception exploded into his consciousness after he witnessed the carnage and devastation of the Front. He saw "the Earth's living envelope—the Biosphere," and then he perceived "totalized Mankind—the Noosphere. But the price I would have to pay for this, if I was to bring it finally and sharply into focus, was no less than the spiritual shock of the War."[2] He believed that this perceptual ability would increase among people, it would evolve, and a growing number of individuals would be able to directly perceive the noosphere, too.

Part of this process, for Chardin, was the human being's recognition of what he described as forms of life called *monads*, or the collective groups that belonged to a higher order than the individual.

"That means that he [a person] *must* coalesce into physical relationships and groupings that belong to a higher order than his. It is, of course, quite impossible for him to apprehend these groupings directly *as such* but there may be indications that enable him to recognize perfectly well their existence and the influences they exercise. This gift or faculty of *perceiving*, without actually *seeing*, the reality and organicity of collective magnitude is still comparatively rare."[3]

Chardin compares this organ or perception to the eye and ear, which provide sight and hearing. Although he has described possessing spiritual senses since childhood, he notes that this sense evolved to its current state in his consciousness through horrors of war. He calls it "a sixth sense."[4]

This brings us, almost full circle, to the work of Ioan P. Couliano, whose theories I discussed in the first chapters. In

Eros and Magic in the Renaissance, he begins the project of restoring our knowledge of the spiritual senses. Like Chardin, he grapples with the question of the duality of matter and the spiritual senses. He begins with Plato and his student, Aristotle.

"Aristotle does not question the existence of the Platonic soul-body dichotomy. But, with an interest in the secrets of nature, he feels the need to define empirically the relations between those two separate entities [spirit and matter]." This brings Aristotle to the idea of "an apparatus, of which the stars are made, and performs the function of resolving the contradiction between the corporeal and the incorporeal." Aristotle calls this sense the "phantasia or inner sense, the sidereal spirit [that] transforms messages from the five senses in phantasms perceptible to the soul."[5]

Couliano goes on to show how the tradition of the spiritual senses shaped Western culture until the nineteenth century. By that point, it had largely disappeared from scholarly discourse, surviving only as what he calls "a mere curiosity of history."[6] Its proper domain—the imagination—did not disappear. Instead, he writes, it became the primary operating system of influence, first for magicians and later for modern advertisers and political propagandists. His work reveals how these sectors effectively replaced religion and, in some cases, came to rival or even supplant governmental institutions. One need not speculate about AI-generated propaganda to see this dynamic at work; it already permeates search engines, advertising ecosystems, and digital media environments.

There is, however, an important distinction between

Couliano's historical analysis of the spiritual senses and the experiential accounts offered by Pierre Teilhard de Chardin and Marshall McLuhan, both of whom wrote about their spiritual senses. For Chardin and McLuhan, as with other sense organs, the spiritual sense apprehends something real. Couliano begins his genealogy with Aristotle, but he does not engage Plato's insistence—voiced through Socrates—on the primacy of the Good as an objective reality that the spiritual senses intuit and apprehend. Couliano demonstrates that one of the most powerful mechanisms of social control is the hijacking of a culture's spiritual senses through the manipulation of imagination. Chardin, McLuhan, and Mark Stahlman, however, insist—again echoing Socrates—that there is something real behind the phantasms of imagination.

What separates these positions, then, is not whether the imagination is powerful, but whether it is ultimately *referential*: whether the spiritual senses are merely instruments to be captured and deployed, or whether they are oriented toward a reality that exceeds them and cannot be reduced to manipulation. Our mythic prophet Jonah stands as a counterexample to purely phantasmic accounts of the spiritual senses, because his encounter with an incomprehensible God results in his resistance, his flight, and ultimately, a confrontation with the reality of his moral obligation.

ACKNOWLEDGMENTS

I would like to thank and acknowledge the many people who have helped and encouraged me during the writing of this book. David Metcalfe has been my colleague and friend for over a decade. He is my co-instructor for my public UFO courses and continues to influence how I think about this topic. I am deeply grateful for his help and support.

I want to acknowledge the substantial influence that Jeff Kripal has had on me, as well as on so many researchers in this field. I would not have had the courage to embark on this research had it not been for Jeff's writings.

I would like to thank the people who directly informed the chapters of this book. Dana has been both an inspiration and a colleague. She alerted me to the work of Julian Jaynes, who wrote about the bicameral mind, and to its relevance for this topic. I also admire her courage. Mark Stahlman called me at precisely the right time and opened my mind to faculty psychology and its history. Once I encountered this framework, my understanding and reading of the works of Pierre Teilhard de Chardin, Marshall McLuhan, and Arthur C. Clarke opened—as Chardin would say—onto a new universe. It is a universe I had long been waiting for and wanting to see. I am grateful to Katie for talking about her transmissions.

I want to thank musician Steven Halpern for helping me with the section of the book devoted to him, which he edited almost entirely. I would like to thank the people of the Invisible College and those who circle its orbit, some of whom can be named and many of whom cannot. They include Jacques Vallée, Hal Puthoff, Karl Nell, Eric Davis, Kit Greene, Peter Skafish, Jonathan Davies, Ross Coulthart, the people who knew Ingo Swann, Jesse Michels, Garry Nolan, Beatriz Villarroel, Whitley Strieber, and Lue Elizondo. There are many more, and they know who they are.

Colleagues and friends have supported and inspired me throughout this work. Leslie Kean's research is definitive in this field, and I am grateful for her comments on my unpublished manuscript. Eric Wargo's theoretical genius has helped me think through anomalous events. Joanna Ebenstein's books and her school continue to influence me. Matthew Roberts, Greg Bishop, Hussein Ali Agrama, Josh Ritter, and Brett Robinson all influenced different aspects of this book. Dr. Aaron French has been a huge support to my work and a resource for information about UFOs and esoteric traditions. Brenda Denzler has been my friend and colleague since the beginning.

I want to thank my editors, who have been extremely helpful and patient. Joel Fotinos believes in this work, and for that I am deeply grateful. The two editors at St. Martin's Essentials were exceptionally helpful in their comments on the manuscript. My literary agent, Giles Anderson, is always thoughtful, patient, and supportive. Producers Harris Fishman and Scott Paskoff suddenly found themselves serving as impromptu editors, and their comments were instrumental. I would also like to especially thank the twenty-year-old AI specialist who edited the manuscript and whose insights into different forms of AI and their capacities for reasoning proved invaluable.

I want to thank my students and young colleagues—Christopher Moreland, Mark Burchick, Jose Hernandez, Joya, and the many students who have taken my non-university courses. I am grateful to the young experiencer who shared her insights. Thank you to Andrew Del Rossi of the American Teilhard Association for his comments on Chardin's work. I would also like to acknowledge my university, the University of North Carolina Wilmington, and my colleagues there, for their support of my work over many years.

Finally, I would like to express my deepest love and gratitude to my family. My two brothers and mother were my first scholarly journey partners, and they have accompanied me on many journeys since. All my work, including this book, is dedicated to my children, and to my husband, Jeff Heath, whose love and support mean everything to me.

NOTES

Introduction

1. Jon. 3:7–8 (New International Version).
2. Jon. 4:10–11 (NIV).
3. Ethan Mollick, *Co-Intelligence: The New Path for Humans and Machines* (Harper Business, 2024), https://commonreads.com/2024/05/21/an-excerpt-from-co-intelligence/; Yuval Noah Harari, *Nexus: A Brief History of Information Networks from the Stone Age to AI* (Fern Press, 2024), as discussed in transcript, "Our AI Future Is Way Worse Than You Think," *Singju Post*, April 22, 2025, https://singjupost.com/transcript-of-our-ai-future-is-way-worse-than-you-think-yuval-noah-harari/.
4. Norbert Wiener, "Some Moral and Technical Consequences of Automation," *Science* 131, no. 3410 (May 6, 1960): 1355–1358, https://www.science.org/doi/10.1126/science.131.3410.1355.

Chapter 1: The Antichrist Algorithm

1. René Girard, *Violence and the Sacred*, trans. Patrick Gregory (Johns Hopkins University Press, 1979).
2. Kathleen Coleman, "Fatal Charades: Roman Executions Staged as Mythological Enactments," *The Journal of Roman Studies* 80 (1990): 44–73, https://doi.org/10.2307/300280.
3. Gil Bailey, "René Girard's Genius and Generosity," *Catholic World Report*, November 5, 2015, https://www.catholicworldreport.com/2015/11/05/rene-girards-genius-and-generosity/.

Chapter 2: Apocalypse

1. Robert Hugh Benson, *Lord of the World* (Sir Isaac Pitman & Sons, 1907), chapter 4, part II.
2. John S. Hutton et al., "Screen Usage Linked to Differences in Brain Structure in Young Children," *Scientific Reports* 12, no. 1 (2022), https://doi.org/10.1038/s41598-022-20922-0.
3. John S. Hutton, "Digital Media and Developing Brains: Concerns and Opportunities," *Current Addiction Reports* 11 (2024): 287–298, https://doi.org/10.1007/s40429-024-00545-3.
4. Eva H. Telzer et al., "Habitual Social Media Checking and Neural Sensitivity to Social Reward in Adolescence," *JAMA Pediatrics* 177, no. 2 (2023), accessed January 3, 2023, https://jamanetwork.com/journals/jamapediatrics/fullarticle/2799812; and Eveline A. Crone and Elly A. Konijn, "Media Use and Brain Development During Adolescence," *Nature Communications* 9 (2018), https://doi.org/10.1038/s41467-018-03126-X.

Chapter 3: The Apocalyptic Event

1. Parts of chapters 3 and 4 of this book, *The Others*, appear in *Religion and the UFO* (Bloomsbury Academic Press, forthcoming), "The Arrival of the Supraterrestrial: Childhood's End in the Era of AI," ed. Aaron French.
2. Ioan P. Couliano, *Eros and Magic in the Renaissance* (Chicago Original Paperback, 1987).
3. Jeffrey Kripal, *Mutants and Mystics: Science Fiction, Superhero Comics, and the Paranormal* (University of Chicago Press, 2011), and personal correspondence.
4. Patrick Parrinder, *Shadows of the Future: H.G. Wells, Science Fiction, and Prophecy* (Liverpool University Press, 1995), 115–126.
5. James F. McGrath, "Science Fiction and Prophecy," *Patheos,* March 18, 2019, https://www.patheos.com/blogs/religionprof/2019/03/science-fiction-and-prophecy.html.
6. Couliano, *Eros and Magic in the Renaissance,* 5.
7. Kripal, *Mutants and Mystics,* and personal correspondence.
8. Arthur C. Clarke, "Extra-Terrestrial Relays: Can Rocket Stations Give World-wide Radio Coverage?," *Wireless World,* October 1945, http://clarkeinstitute.org/wp-content/uploads/2010/04/ClarkeWirelessWorldArticle.pdf.
9. John Uri, "Arthur C. Clarke—Prophet of the Space Age," January 2018, https://ntrs.nasa.gov/api/citations/20180006504/downloads/20180006504.pdf. Clarifies Clarke's geospatial satellite designation.

10. Marshall McLuhan, *Understanding Media: The Extensions of Man* (McGraw-Hill, 1964), 7; Marshall McLuhan, *The Gutenberg Galaxy: The Making of Typographic Man* (University of Toronto Press, 1962), 31, 32, 43.
11. Marshall McLuhan, "The Gadget Lover: Narcissus as Narcosis," *Explorations* 8 (1957): 3–11; McLuhan, *The Gutenberg Galaxy.*
12. Marshall McLuhan, in "Marshall McLuhan Interview from *Playboy,* 1969," ed. Philip Rogaway, for UC Davis's ECS 188, Ethics in an Age of Technology, 1994 edited version of "The *Playboy* Interview: Marshall McLuhan," *Playboy* (March 1969): 15, https://web.cs.ucdavis.edu/~rogaway/classes/188/spring07/mcluhan.pdf.
13. McLuhan, in Rogaway, "Interview from *Playboy,*" 18.
14. Dante Alighieri, *Paradiso,* vol. 3 of *The Divine Comedy,* trans. Charles S. Singleton (Princeton University Press, 1975), I.70–72.

Chapter 4: The Child Network

1. Marshall McLuhan, in "Marshall McLuhan Interview from *Playboy,* 1969," ed. Philip Rogaway, for UC Davis's ECS 188, Ethics in an Age of Technology, 1994 edited version of "The *Playboy* Interview: Marshall McLuhan," *Playboy* (March 1969): 3, https://web.cs.ucdavis.edu/~rogaway/classes/188/spring07/mcluhan.pdf.
2. McLuhan, in Rogaway, "Interview from *Playboy,*" 12–13.
3. McLuhan, in Rogaway, "Interview from *Playboy,*" 15.
4. McLuhan, in Rogaway, "Interview from *Playboy,*" 18.
5. Arthur C. Clarke, *Childhood's End* (Del Rey Books, 1990), 68.
6. Clarke, *Childhood's End,* 135.
7. Clarke, *Childhood's End,* 135.
8. Clarke, *Childhood's End,* 19.
9. McLuhan, in Rogaway, "Interview from *Playboy,*" 17.
10. Clarke, *Childhood's End,* 62.
11. Aldous Huxley, *Brave New World Revisited* (Harper & Row, 1958), xviii–xix.
12. Clarke, *Childhood's End,* 61.
13. Clarke, *Childhood's End,* 61.
14. McLuhan, in Rogaway, "Interview from *Playboy,*" 19.
15. Clarke, *Childhood's End,* 62.
16. Clarke, *Childhood's End,* 63.
17. McLuhan, in Rogaway, "Interview from *Playboy,*" 12.

18. Clarke, *Childhood's End*, 93.
19. Clarke, *Childhood's End*, 209.
20. McLuhan, in Rogaway, "Interview from *Playboy*," 15.
21. Clarke, *Childhood's End*, 196.
22. Clarke, *Childhood's End*, unnumbered front matter.

Chapter 5: "Extraordinary Claims" Revisited

1. Michael Bess and Diana Walsh Pasulka, eds., *Posthumanism: The Future of Homo Sapiens* (Macmillan Reference USA, 2018).
2. Meta Fundamental AI Research and Basque Center on Cognition, Brain and Language, "Brain-to-Text Decoding: A Non-Invasive Approach via Typing," *Meta AI Research blog*, February 6–7, 2025, https://ai.meta.com/research/publications/brain-to-text-decoding-a-non-invasive-approach-via-typing/.
3. Arthur C. Clarke, "Hazards of Prophecy: The Failure of Imagination," in *Profiles of the Future: An Inquiry into the Limits of the Possible* (Harper & Row, 1962), 36.
4. Arthur C. Clarke, *Childhood's End* (Del Rey Books, 1990). While paranormal events pervade the book, in particular see the seance scene on 118–128.
5. Neil McAleer, *Arthur C. Clarke: The Authorized Biography* (Bantam Press, 1992), quoted in "Arthur C. Clarke," *Wikipedia*, accessed December 14, 2025, https://en.wikipedia.org/wiki/Arthur_C._Clarke.
6. Eric Wargo, *From Nowhere: Artists, Writers, and the Precognitive Imagination* (Anomalist Books, 2024). Wargo presents evidence and reasoning to support revealing connections between precognition and the creative imagination.
7. Albert Einstein, letter to Max Born, March 3, 1947, in *The Born–Einstein Letters: Correspondence between Albert Einstein and Max and Hedwig Born, 1916–1955*, ed. Max Born, trans. Irene Born, with commentaries (Macmillan, 1971), 158.
8. Clarke, *Childhood's End*, 63.
9. Clarke, *Childhood's End*, 201.
10. Clarke, *Childhood's End*, 95.
11. Marshall McLuhan, in "Marshall McLuhan Interview from *Playboy*, 1969," ed. Philip Rogaway, for UC Davis's ECS 188, Ethics in an Age of Technology, 1994 edited version of "The *Playboy* Interview: Marshall McLuhan," *Playboy* (March 1969): 18, https://web.cs.ucdavis.edu/~rogaway/classes/188/spring07/mcluhan.pdf.

12. McLuhan, in Rogaway, "Interview from *Playboy*," 20.
13. McLuhan, in Rogaway, "Interview from *Playboy*," 15.
14. Marshall McLuhan, "Extra Sensory Perception Is Normal Perception," *McLuhan's New Sciences: Notes on the Media as Environment*, accessed December 13, 2025, https://mcluhansnewsciences.com/mcluhan/2023/07/e-s-p/.
15. McLuhan, in Rogaway, "Interview from *Playboy*," 5.
16. Wargo, *From Nowhere*, 306.
17. Wargo, *From Nowhere*, 69–70.

Chapter 6: The Digital Sphere and the Rise of the Androids

1. Mark Stahlman, Brett Robinson, Peter Berkman, and Adam Pugen, "Making Sense of a World in Transition," *Church Life Journal*, January 11, 2021, https://churchlifejournal.nd.edu/articles/making-sense-of-a-world-in-transition/.
2. Norbert Wiener, *The Human Use of Human Beings: Cybernetics and Society—A Profound Examination of AI, Cybernetics, and the Human-Machine Relationship, Anticipating the Dilemmas of Modern Technology and Neuroscience* (HarperCollins), 43. Kindle.
3. Wiener, *The Human Use of Human Beings*, 198.
4. Norbert Wiener, *God & Golem, Inc.: A Comment on Certain Points Where Cybernetics Impinges on Religion* (Da Capo Press, 1989).
5. Shrikant Rangnekar, host, *52 Living Ideas*, podcast, February 25, 2022, https://52livingideas.com/2022/02/25/digital-catholic-social-teaching-the-church-technology-by-mark-stahlman-a-scribal-hyperbook/.
6. Rangnekar, *52 Living Ideas*, February 25, 2022.
7. Elizabeth Englander, "Teens are Flocking to AI Chatbots. Is this Healthy?," *Scientific American*, August 12, 2025, https://www.scientificamerican.com/article/teens-are-flocking-to-ai-chatbots-is-this-healthy/.
8. Arthur C. Clarke, *Childhood's End* (Del Rey Books, 1990), 62.
9. Aristotle, *De Anima* (*On the Soul*), De Anima III.1–2 (425a27–426b8).
10. Thomas Aquinas, "Commentary on Aristotle's De Anima," trans. Kenelm Foster and Silvester Humphries (Yale University Press, 1951).

Chapter 7: Marshall McLuhan's Spiritual Sense

1. Marshall McLuhan, *Understanding Media: The Extensions of Man* (McGraw-Hill, 1964), 3.

2. Eric McLuhan, introduction to *The Medium and the Light: Reflections on Religion*, by Marshall McLuhan, eds. Eric McLuhan and Jacek Szklarek (Stoddart, 1999), xiv.
3. Marshall McLuhan, *The Medium and the Light, Reflections on Religion*, eds. Eric McLuhan and Jacek Szklarek (Stoddart, 1999), 95.
4. Marshall McLuhan, *The Medium and the Light*, 95.
5. Mark Stahlman, personal correspondence.
6. Marshall McLuhan, *The Medium and the Light*, 203–209.
7. Marshall McLuhan, *The Medium and the Light*, 72.
8. Quoted by Jenny James Taylor, "Facebook and the Anti-Christ," October 7, 2021, https://jennytaylor.media/2021/10/07/facebook-and-the-anti-christ/.
9. These studies are cited in chapter 2 of this book.

Chapter 8: A Rival Star: Pierre Teilhard de Chardin's Sci-Fi Theology

1. Pierre Teilhard de Chardin, *The Phenomenon of Man*, trans. Bernard Wall (Harper & Brothers, 1959), 182–183. It is unclear to me who originally coined the term. The concept of the noosophere was articulated by Édouard Le Roy, in "L'avenir de l'esprit humain," *Revue de philosophie* 47 (1927): 400–420. The concept is also associated with Vladimir Vernadsky in *The Biosphere* (Librairie Félix Alcan, 1926). These men were colleagues of Chardin's.
2. Pope Benedict XVI, "Celebration of Vespers with the Faithful of Aosta," Homily, July 24, 2009, https://www.vatican.va/content/benedict-xvi/en/homilies/2009/documents/hf_ben-xvi_hom_20090724_vespri-aosta.html.
3. Chardin, *The Phenomenon of Man*, 31.
4. Pierre Teilhard de Chardin, *The Future of Man* (Harper & Row, 1959), 164.
5. Chardin, *The Future of Man*, 165.
6. Chardin, *The Future of Man*, https://www.religion-online.org/book-chapter/chapter-7-a-great-event-foreshadowed-the-planetization-of-mankind/.
7. Pierre Teilhard de Chardin, *The Heart of Matter* (Harcourt, 1978). In this book Chardin makes the case for the nonduality of matter and spirit.
8. Chardin, *The Heart of Matter*, 17.
9. Chardin, *The Heart of Matter*, 17.
10. Chardin, *The Heart of Matter*, 17.
11. Chardin, *The Heart of Matter*, 25.
12. Chardin, *The Heart of Matter*, 26.

13. Chardin, *The Heart of Matter*, 26.
14. Chardin, *The Heart of Matter*, 31.
15. Chardin, *The Heart of Matter*, 78nn11–12.
16. Cornelia C. Walther, "Is AI Taking Us to the Heart of the Noosphere?," *Forbes*, June 2025, https://www.forbes.com/sites/corneliawalther/2025/06/17/is-ai-taking-us-to-the-heart-of-the-noosphere/.
17. Robert Wright, "Artificial Intelligence and the Noosphere," *NonZero Newsletter*, June 28, 2023, https://www.nonzero.org/p/artificial-intelligence-and-the-noosphere.

Chapter 9: The Ultra-Human and the Transfigured Body

1. Matt. 27:50–54 (New International Version).
2. 2 Cor. 11:26 (NIV).
3. Rom. 8:35 (NIV).
4. Phil. 3:20–21 (NIV).
5. 1 Cor. 15:35 (NIV).
6. Pierre Teilhard de Chardin, *Writings in Time of War*, 55, https://archive.org/details/writingsintimeof00teil/.
7. Pierre Teilhard de Chardin, "Cosmic Life," in *Hymn of the Universe*, trans. Simon Barrows (Harper & Row, 1965), 60.
8. Chardin, *Writings in Time of War*, 47.
9. Chardin, *Writings in Time of War*, 63.
10. Chardin, *Writings in Time of War*, 55.
11. Matt. 6:29 (NIV).
12. Chardin, *Writings in Time of War*, 55.
13. Chardin, "Cosmic Life," April 24, 1916, The Library of Consciousness, https://www.organism.earth/library/document/cosmic-life.
14. David J. Halperin, *The Faces of the Chariot: Early Jewish Responses to Ezekiel's Vision* (1988), where he sets out the mystical tradition, and his later works on UFOs (e.g., *Intimate Alien: The Hidden Story of the UFO*, 2020), where he explicitly compares UFOs to the Merkabah; Jeffrey J. Kripal, *Authors of the Impossible: The Paranormal and the Sacred* (University of Chicago Press, 2010), which traces the continuity between mystical ascent traditions and UFO narratives; and Carl Raschke, *The Interruption of Eternity: Modern Gnosticism and the Origins of the New Religious Consciousness* (Nelson-Hall, 1980), where UFOs are read as a new form of the visionary tradition.
15. Pierre Teilhard de Chardin, *The Heart of Matter* (Harcourt, 1978), 67.
16. Chardin, *The Heart of Matter*, 74.

17. Chardin, *The Heart of Matter*, 73.
18. Chardin, *The Heart of Matter*, 76–77.
19. Raschke, *The Interruption of Eternity*, 200–210; Kripal, *Authors of the Impossible*; Jeffrey J. Kripal, *The Superhumanities: Historical Precedents, Moral Objections, New Realities* (University of Chicago Press, 2022).
20. Chardin.

Chapter 10: Gilgamesh's Common Task

1. Nikolai Fedorov, *The Philosophy of the Common Task*, trans. Elisabeth Koutaissoff and Marilyn Minto, ed. Boris Jakim (Nordland Publishing Company, 1979).
2. George Pendle, *Strange Angel: The Otherworldly Life of Rocket Scientist John Whiteside Parsons* (Harcourt, 2005).
3. George M. Young, *The Russian Cosmists: The Esoteric Futurism of Nikolai Fedorov and His Followers* (Oxford University Press, 2012).
4. Pierre Teilhard de Chardin, *The Divine Millieu: An Essay on the Interior Life*, trans. Bernard Wall (Harper & Row, 1960), 143.
5. *The Letters of Teilhard De Chardin and Lucile Swan*, edited by Mary Wood Gilbert and Thomas M. King (Georgetown University Press, 1993), 72–73.
6. Nikolai Fedorov, *What Was Man Created For? The Philosophy of the Common Task*, trans. Elisabeth Koutaissoff and Marilyn Minto (1990), 128.
7. Aleksander Sukhovo-Kobylin, quoted in George Young, *The Russian Cosmists*, 18.
8. Dante Alighieri, *Paradiso*, in *The Divine Comedy*, trans. Allen Mandelbaum (Bantam Books, 1986), Canto 1, lines 70–72.
9. Alighieri, *Paradiso*, Canto 30, lines 18–21.
10. Alighieri, *Paradiso*, Canto 33, lines 142–145.
11. *Black Mirror*, season 2, episode 1, "Be Right Back," written by Charlie Brooker, directed by Owen Harris, aired February 11, 2013, on United Kingdom Channel 4 and later on Netflix.
12. Roselyne Min with AFP, "Rise of China's 'Ghost Bots': This Father Turned to AI to 'Digitally Revive' His Dead Son," *EuroNews* December 19, 2023, updated December 21, 2023, https://www.euronews.com/next/2023/12/19/rise-of-chinas-ghost-bots-this-father-turned-to-ai-to-digitally-revive-his-dead-son.
13. Hani Richter, "It Feels Like, Almost, He's Here," Reuters, September 13, 2025, https://www.reuters.com/lifestyle/it-feels-like-almost-hes-here-how-ai-is-changing-way-we-grieve-2025-09-13/.

14. Julian De Freitas et al., "Lessons from an App Update at Replika AI: Identity Discontinuity in Human-AI Relationships," Harvard Business School Working Paper no. 25–018, October 2024, https://arxiv.org/abs/2412.14190?utm_source=chatgpt.com.
15. Parts of this chapter have been published in Diana Pasulka, "Virtual Religion: Popular Culture and the Digital World," in *Religion: Sources, Perspectives, and Methodologies*, ed. J. J. Kripal (Macmillan Reference USA, 2016), 325–342.
16. Ray Kurzweil, *The Singularity Is Near: When Humans Transcend Biology* (Viking, 2005), 7.

Chapter 11: An American Cosmist

1. D. W. Pasulka, *American Cosmic: UFOs, Religion, Technology* (Oxford University Press, 2019).
2. The material in this chapter is from interviews with Dana and from her unpublished manuscript about her experience.
3. Dana's unpublished manuscript, 10.
4. Julian Huxley, *New Bottles for New Wine* (Chatto and Windus, 1957).
5. Dana's unpublished manuscript, 10.

Chapter 12: New Light from the Black Hole

1. Timothy Leary, "Starseed: Transmitted from Folsom Prison," https://archive.org/details/starseed00learrich.
2. Leary, "Starseed," 10.
3. Leary, "Starseed," 10–11.
4. Leary, "Starseed," 18.
5. Leary, "Starseed," 8.
6. Matthew Roberts, personal correspondence, March 27, 2023.
7. This is cowritten by Steven Halpern.
8. David Metcalfe, "The History and Origin of the Starseed People," April 30, 2021, https://kemono.cr/patreon/user/4598320/post/50683763.
9. David Metcalfe, "Star Children and Psychic Futures," presentation.
10. Gus Thomson, "1978's UFO sightings over Loomis, Auburn," *Gold Country Media*, October 28, 2019, https://goldcountrymedia.com/news/150351/1978s-ufo-sightings-over-loomis-auburn/.
11. Pierre Teilhard de Chardin, *The Divine Millieu: An Essay on the Interior Life*, trans. Bernard Wall (Harper & Row, 1960), 147.
12. Metcalfe, "The History and Origin of the Starseed People."

13. John Keel, *The Eighth Tower: On Ultraterrestrials and the Superspectrum* (Anomalist Books), 146. Kindle.
14. Keel, *The Eighth Tower*, 131.
15. Keel, *The Eighth Tower*, 199–200.

Chapter 13: Rival Stars

1. Max Weber, "Science as a Vocation," in *From Max Weber: Essays in Sociology*, trans. and eds. H. H. Gerth and C. Wright Mills (Oxford University Press, 1946), 129–156. Weber gave a public lecture in 1917 of the same name, and this essay is based on that lecture at the University of Munich for the group Freistudentischer Bund.
2. Steven J. Dick, *Plurality of Worlds: The Origins of the Extraterrestrial Life Debate from Democritus to Kant* (Cambridge University Press, 2012).
3. Steven J. Dick, "The Postbiological Universe Revisited: Cultural Evolution in the Cosmos," in *Origin of Life and the New Science of Astrobiology: Uniting the Natural Sciences, Social Sciences, and Humanities through Astrobiology*, eds. O. A. Chon Torres and J. Seckbach (Wiley-Scrivener, forthcoming). Much of this information is also in the published book by Steven J. Dick, *Space, Time, and Aliens: Collected Works on Cosmos and Culture* (Springer Nature, 2020).
4. Dick, "The Postbiological Universe Revisited." Throughout the essay Dick argues for this point.
5. Dick, "The Postbiological Universe Revisited," 9.
6. Dick, "The Postbiological Universe Revisited," 5.
7. Kevin N. Laland, *Darwin's Unfinished Symphony: How Culture Made the Human Mind* (Princeton University Press, 2017), referenced by Dick, "The Postbiological Universe Revisited," 6.
8. Nick Bostrom, *Superintelligence: Paths, Dangers, Strategies* (Oxford University Press, 2014). Dick references Bostrom's argument in "The Postbiological Universe Revisited," 2–8.
9. Dick, "The Postbiological Universe Revisited," 13.
10. Dick, "The Postbiological Universe Revisited," 13.

Chapter 14: The Other 1960s

1. The testimonies come from the lay Catholic devotional documentary "Garabandal Warning: Our Ladys Messages and Prophecies," https://www.youtube.com/watch?v=-tCAwgmmTuk&t.
2. "Garabandal Warning" (italics added).

3. "Garabandal Warning."
4. "Garabandal Warning."
5. "Garabandal Warning."
6. "Garabandal Warning."
7. "Garabandal Warning."
8. "Garabandal Warning."
9. "Garabandal Warning."
10. "Garabandal Warning."
11. "Garabandal Warning."
12. "Garabandal Warning."
13. "Garabandal Warning."
14. Pierre Teilhard de Chardin, *The Heart of Matter* (Harcourt, 1978), 78n11.
15. Mark Stahlman, conversation.
16. News Nation, "Reality Check: UAP Retrieval Whistleblower & Dr. Garry Nolan on Injury Claims," https://www.youtube.com/watch?v=HylFTLt0mEE.

Postscript: The Control Mechanism

1. Conversation with Katie, December 18, 2025.
2. Pierre Teilhard de Chardin, *The Heart of Matter* (Harcourt, 1978), 29.
3. Chardin, *The Heart of Matter*, 31, italics are mine.
4. Chardin, *The Heart of Matter*, 31.
5. Ioan P. Couliano, *Eros and Magic in the Renaissance* (Chicago Original Paperback, 1987), 5.
6. Couliano, *Eros and Magic in the Renaissance*, 5.

ABOUT THE AUTHOR

J. Heath

D. W. Pasulka is a professor of religious studies at the University of North Carolina Wilmington. She has written acclaimed books that focus on religion, technology, and emerging religious movements and has published journal articles and book chapters that delve into the connection between technologies and religious practices and beliefs.

Pasulka has appeared on popular podcasts like *The Joe Rogan Experience*, *Lex Fridman*, and *Mysterious Universe* and in mainstream media such as *The New York Times* and *The Guardian*. She was the consulting producer for the Emmy-nominated Amblin Netflix series *Encounters* and the consultant for the first movie in the Conjuring franchise (2013). Her insights were also featured in the J. J. Abrams–produced docuseries *UFO*.